P9-AFI-144

Public Library

Advance Praise for

ALL DOWN DARKNESS WIDE

"Stunning . . . A profoundly moving meditation on queer identity, mental illness, and the fragility of life."
—*Kirkus Reviews* (starred)

"A raw and hypnotic retelling reminiscent of Garth Greenwell's *Cleanness* . . . an exquisite vision of queer heartbreak and liberation." —*Publishers Weekly*

"Gorgeous and moving prose that excavates the deep complexities of grief, shame and love with a tenderness and lightness of touch that make the words sing."
—Andrew McMillan, author of *Physical*

"It's impossible not to be intensely moved by this book, written with a poet's eye for detail: line after line that grip head and heart. You are truly there with Seán Hewitt in the darkness and the light." —Niven Govinden, author of *Diary of a Film*

"Hewitt's gorgeous prose gleams like a dayspring in the dimness, his story lingering long after the book is closed."
—Melissa Harrison, author of *All Among the Barley*

"I loved the complexity of it, the way he subtly reveals how our fragile identities are formed (and de-formed) by the forces that surround us." —Charlie Gilmour, author of *Featherhood*

"Luminous and utterly original, a book with its own darkly beautiful gravity." —Niamh Campbell, author of *This Happy*

ALSO BY SEÁN HEWITT

Tongues of Fire

J.M. Synge: Nature, Politics, Modernism

ALL
DOWN
DARKNESS
WIDE

A MEMOIR

Seán Hewitt

PENGUIN PRESS NEW YORK 2022

PENGUIN PRESS
An imprint of Penguin Random House LLC
penguinrandomhouse.com

Copyright © 2022 by Seán Hewitt
Penguin Random House supports copyright. Copyright fuels creativity,
encourages diverse voices, promotes free speech, and creates a vibrant culture.
Thank you for buying an authorized edition of this book and for complying with
copyright laws by not reproducing, scanning, or distributing any part of it in any
form without permission. You are supporting writers and allowing Penguin
Random House to continue to publish books for every reader.

"Min ångest är en risig skog," poem by Pär Lagerkvist – licensed
through © Pär Lagerkvist Estate, SWEDEN.

ISBN 9780593300084 (hardcover)
ISBN 9780593300091 (ebook)

Printed in the United States of America
1st Printing

ALL

DOWN

DARKNESS

WIDE

I

The Oratory of St James's Cemetery in Liverpool has no windows along the whole length of its outer walls. Only a long rectangular skylight, its leaded panes half-mossed over, lets the winter sun reach down and touch the white marble statues staring blankly inside. A mortuary chapel, but long closed up, its coffered ceiling and tall, carved columns are mostly in shadow. Years ago, as the great homes of the city were pulled down stone by stone, the monuments of proud families (monuments of terracotta and marble and bronze) were hoisted here and locked away, and so the wealth of the city – wrenched from far-off lands and furnished from blood – was hidden, and so forgotten.

And as the years went by, other things were hidden, too. Some (like the terraced slums of the poor and their wash-houses) were razed, others (the orphanages and workhouses, the asylums and homes for the destitute) were emptied one by one, turned by sharp-suited businessmen into flats or bars or restaurants, where the names of the dead, engraved in plaques on newly pointed walls, were the climbing holds of a city once again dragging itself up out of its own grave. And so the churches and crypts were closed, and the docks shut down, and the shackles shipped and left on other shores, and the subterranean tunnels and the catacombs were filled in with stones, and the quarry was planted with oaks and with sycamores and with the bodies of the dead. And it was in this way that the ghosts of the city were parcelled off, ushered from the streets into derelict buildings, made to stand in exhibition cases, hurried into the pages of books and diaries, and folded away. For, after all, ghosts can only live in the darkness; and once the dark places are closed up, their cast-iron locks bolted fast, it is easy for those who do not live with them to pretend that ghosts do not exist at all.

Past midnight, one mid-January, standing in the church gardens, I felt the wind blow up from the River Mersey, weighted with Atlantic salt. It blustered up to the city, battering the red bricks of the warehouses on the dock, rattling the barred doors of the pump-house and the locks of the customs house. I heard it rush south-east between the empty units along St James's Street, clapping the tattered flags of the old sailors' church, and spinning frantically in the bell-turret of St Vincent's. It rushed up the steep junction of Parliament Street, past the new-builds, over the waiting cars at the traffic lights, and there scurried down the tree-tunnelled sandstone path into the cathedral cemetery, resting, finally, in a swirl of leaves and a ripple of the spring water by the catacombs, unseen by anyone except a carved angel weeping over a nineteenth-century grave, and the lone figure of a man – me – kneeling and drinking from the water flowing in runnels down the old cemetery wall.

I had come here to meet someone – a man I didn't know, but who was somehow like myself. Above the cemetery gardens the terrifying neo-gothic cathedral loomed across the sky, its stained glass half-aglow even at night. I could almost feel the weight of its shadow, like a body bearing down on mine. To venture into the graveyard, you have first to walk through a tunnel of hollowed rock, its walls lined with old grave-slabs and dripping with dank water filtered through the paving stones and tree roots overhead. And at the end of this, where hardly any light can be found after sundown, a little path winds fearlessly onwards between the holly and the yews and the leaning granite obelisks.

Nearly a century has passed since the last body was interred here, and the lichen has spread over the tombs and into the once-neat etchings of names and dates and Latin mottos and platitudes both sentimental and heartfelt. Lichen over the staunch Victorian formalities of lives lived in stoicism and resignation, and into the carefully chosen testaments to numberless tragedies and joys given from mother to child, from husband to wife, from friend to friend and from lover to dearly missed lover. Years ago, a hearse tunnel, now capped with brick, brought carriages, one by one, down from the Georgian grandeur of Rodney Street into the cemetery, and now perhaps no one is old enough to remember these dead.

At the centre of the cemetery, flowing down into a square pool between the laid-out gravestones, a little spring uncovered in the eighteenth century runs on, unperturbed, trickling over the luminous green growths of liverwort and algae on the bricked-up far wall of the plot. And on this January night, when the only living inhabitant of the graveyard is a single man drinking from the spring, anyone might come down and walk under the silvered boughs, hearing that gentle babbling stream, and imagine all the souls here, cooped up in the soil, passing from root to root, moving slowly in the underworld of the earth. At the heart of it all is water – its slow leak along the walls, its passage through all the plants and mosses and trees, its movement through the apertures of the shale embankments, its sheening under the moon on the marble of a family vault. Laden with iron, the water is sharp and metallic and tastes faintly of blood. Some in the city believe in its healing powers, and follow the words of the inscription carved above the spring, which speaks, in the voice of water, of the endless cycle of giving:

> Christian reader view in me
> An emblem of true charity,
> Who freely what I have bestow
> Though neither heard nor seen to flow.

I, like others, held closer to a different truth: that the water contains the souls of the dead, trapped in the graveyard, and that it turns black, like blood, when boiled.

Ghosts in the water, ghosts in the blood. Everything, once you start to look, is haunted. And so perhaps it was fitting that I came here that evening, unsure of where else to go, feeling lonely and shut out from the daylight world, the downward paths from Princes Park leading me on into this navel of the city. An unsettling place to be after dark, not so much for any fear of the dead, but of the living: the men I had seen huddling around a lighter, their square of tinfoil glinting; the occasional hunched figure wandering; a group of drunks walking the pavement of Hope Street, faces hot with wine. It would be tempting to say that it was a sense of communion that drew me into the gardens, a sense that down here, with the dead, was where I belonged – hollowed out, tired, looking for something in this wooded grove squat amongst the townhouses and the busy roads – but other urges drove me, too, on to the little spring, like a pilgrim to the underworld, my phone's light held up to the darkness, my golden bough.

I met the man by the Huskisson monument. Unsure at first (who can tell if the lone man in the cemetery is the man you're looking for, or the man you don't want to find?), I leant against the bare wall of the tomb and feigned nonchalance, scuffing my heels into the mud. It was only two weeks since I had taken my boyfriend Elias to the airport for the last time. I had lived with him in Sweden, and he had fallen into a deep depression, one that went unchecked for too long. That depression dragged me in, too, proliferated into my life; and here I was, still in the middle of it, so numbed I was barely aware of its presence. After nearly five years, struggling through, we finally admitted that what we had could not be fixed. Too much damage had been done between us. We had been wrecked. It was as though a force had come through the world, alighted on us, and conducted its strike to the ground. Saying goodbye, a fortnight ago, he barely cried as we hugged in the car park, but I was beside myself. I watched him walk off, trailing his suitcase, as the doors of the terminal opened then closed around him. Afterwards, I went to the woods just behind the airport and walked and walked, sitting by the streams and the waterfalls, lifting my head occasionally to say a pained 'Good morning' to the passing walkers, taking the wet bodies of their dogs between my palms and stroking them as the tears streamed down my face. I remember two children running madly among the old oaks, putting their heads into the hollows of the trunks and shouting 'Hello!' 'Hello!' 'Hello!' from the depths of their lungs, as though the god of the tree might wake up and answer them. Here, perhaps, I was doing the same thing: in a cemetery at night, meeting a man I didn't know. Shouting into the hollow trunk of the world and hoping to see a face appear, to feel its touch, to hear its deep, sonorous reply.

The man was tall, his body taut beneath his winter coat and jeans. A kickboxing teacher, it turned out. Later, he would text me, asking if my name was Ryan. He had mistaken (whether accidentally or wilfully, I can't tell) my face in the dark for that of one of his students. I suppose we are all, at some point, taking the face of some ideal lover into our mind and placing it like a mask on to the person in front of us. Maybe I was mistaking him, too, for another boy I once knew. Maybe this was my way of continuing his life, seeing him age into manhood, seeing him inhabit years he never would. If I closed my eyes, perhaps it was Jack I was with, or Elias, or another boy, or all of them merged into a new form.

After some quiet introductions, he nodded towards a thicket of trees and started walking, keeping his distance. I heard the clicking of his lighter as he lit a cigarette, watched him take a deep, slow drag and then exhale the blue smoke into the night-blue air. Then, as I reached him, fumbling: the belt unbuckled, the vertical sound of the zipper. All the time that I was on my knees, I could hear the trembling chain of the spring water clinking and splashing over the far stones. When he finished, I took him all the way into my mouth and held him there as I felt him weaken, then pull back.

Afterwards, I walked to the spring and cupped the ice-cold water into my palm, watched its bright dancing for a second and then lifted it to rinse my mouth. I could still taste him there and couldn't face the long walk home without this little ablution, cleansing myself back into sanctity. As I walked away, up to the Parliament Street gate, I cast my head down, determined to muster some deep reserve of what I thought of as masculine courage. I wanted so much to be the man who could walk in these places at night, to be the man who would not turn his head to check if, in the black spaces of the cemetery, there wasn't a lone figure following, hiding behind the headstones, who might (out of his own fear) stop me from leaving.

A week later I sat up in bed and felt my neck sore and swollen, my glands puffed up and beating. The sun touched each bead of water on my single-paned window, glittering them. I could almost feel the virus pricking and spreading in my body. I panicked. I sweated cold and then hot. My mind whirred and whirred madly over statistics and history, ancestry, all those men lining the corridors of wards, all those bleeping machines and frail, stick-thin corpses. Though I did not know them, their ghosts haunt me. I am, somehow, their descendant: I arrived into a world full of ghosts, and owed a part of myself to each of them. At the clinic, as the nurse took a vial of blood from my arm and commented on the raised width of my vein, she noted down my history, and I heard their voices, and felt a dull weight come over me that wouldn't lift for a week.

In the end it was a false alarm. All clear. Of course it was. I was anxious, full of shame, always expecting the worst, always expecting to be put in line by some sort of cosmic justice. I still saw my body as a thing that might register every misdemeanour and then punish me for them. But it was strange how, in that strip-lit hospital room, my history was not mine at all. Like a river, spreading through its bends and tributaries, it moved through even the most secret parts of my body. It included every encounter, every man, and from there all of their men, all of their encounters, spreading outwards and outwards over the city, then the country, then continents, linking thousands of us together by what we had given to each other, and what we had taken. That night in the cemetery was just one node in a huge, sprawling network. History seeping from one man into the warm body of another, then being carried off into the daily life of the world, barely noticed.

*

It was at school, aged seventeen, that I first became aware of my blood as somehow historical, extending back before I was born. Though I had known it in different ways as a child, I was carrying the weight of the past in my veins. Every day, without thought, my heart pumped it around my body – it seemed natural, unconscious, free from moral-ity. It was only later that I found out that my blood could be a clamp, could be tightened to hold me in place. My high school sat on the edge of a wealthy village by a post-industrial town in the north-west of England. Partly because of its proximity to the town, it was the sort of place where purity (of class, of race, of family) was prized, but left largely unspoken. The village – with its quaint sandstone buildings and bridges, its pubs, its odd festivals, its pretty canal dotted lazily with painted narrowboats – was exclu-sive even to those who schooled there. Catching the bus into school each morning was enough to mark you as an outsider, hailing from some close but far-off place where the house prices were lower, the vowels slightly more lengthened. Wearing the wrong shoes, the cheap blazer, the hand-me-down sports gear – anything was enough to elicit a look or a comment.

Being who I was, I had learnt from a young age the stealth tactics of conformity: how to hide a lisp, how to correct a too-expressive walk, how to pitch my voice lower, which I practised in my bedroom for many weeks during puberty. But it wasn't until I was seventeen that I was faced, consciously, with a non-conformity I couldn't finesse my way out of. I saw then, more clearly than before, the ways in which the world had placed me – even before I knew it – into innate opposition. One afternoon, the blood-donation vans rolled up into the school car park, and suddenly the lunchtime common room was full of nurses and camp beds and middle-class moral fervour. A vague rumour went around the school – a sense of excitement and obligation, a sixth-form rite of passage into adulthood taking place in the oddly transfigured hall. Known as the 'hexagon' for its six-sided structure, the common room was brightly lit, blue, and full of fold-down furniture and tables stacked against the walls. In one corner, there was a small hatch where canteen staff would sell cakes and pastries to teenagers who seemed hardly ever to gain weight. But now, booths had been set up using felt-board dividers, and in each sat a nurse, with a clipboard on her lap and an empty chair in front of her. One by one, we moved from the queue and took our seat in front of whichever nurse was free, and on doing so we were welcomed kindly, and handed a form to fill out. It was a good thing we were doing, it was selfless and right, and they reminded us of that often.

On the form there was a row of tiny boxes, and next to each box was a question. As usual, I went down the list, cavalierly ticking 'no'. No, I do not have HIV. No, I have never been given money for sex. No, I have never injected drugs. And then a pause, a sudden flush of the cheeks. I felt my ears burn red and looked up, wondering if the nurse had noticed my hesitation. 'In the last twelve months,' the form asked, 'have you had oral or anal sex with a man, with or without a condom?' I didn't know what to do. Tell the truth, tick 'yes' and have to leave, have to explain to her and to everyone why I couldn't donate (sixteen, fumbling of zips in the back row of the cinema, something secret and forbidden); or lie, preserve myself as respectable, virginal; a queer, yes, but not the sort of queer who would dream of doing what half the other students did every weekend on the faded couches at the back of the Rugby Club discos. I had changed my accent, studied hard, cultivated myself into inviolability. And so, for everything I had worked for, for the safety of my one-man kingdom, I scratched a quick pencil line through the box that said 'no', and handed the clipboard back to the nurse.

After she pricked my finger and the bright droplet of blood floated in the green vial she was holding, she prepared the soft skin of my inner arm, lay me down on to one of the beds and took out her needle. I felt a flutter in my vein, as though a butterfly were trapped inside. 'Sorry – I caught the valve,' the nurse said, smiling apologetically as I winced. She slid the needle backwards slightly, then pushed it inside again. Assured that my heart would pump out a pint of blood in a short time, the nurse left me lying there and went back to her seat and to the next teenager in line. As I looked up, a dozen of my schoolfriends were lying in a circle of beds, each with a silver needle tucked into their arm, each unconsciously pumping their blood into a clear pint bag, which was held at the side of the bed and rocked rhythmically to keep the blood from clotting or congealing. All around me, as Elvis Presley's 'Good Luck Charm' played from a portable analogue radio, my classmates were lying in silence, staring up at the ceiling tiles, the scarlet pouches of blood moving in iambs, the motion of their hearts externalised and made visible. I watched as each rocked back and forth. It was as though the room was suddenly underwater – the air limpid, strangely beautiful and unnerving. Each thing had a heavy motion; and each person was oddly quiet, slowed by this pre-natal rhythm, the systole and diastole of their own body pulsing out their blood.

Everything felt uncanny – spiritual, almost, and distant. Every so often the nurses in their white coats would move around us, our eyes following them curiously until they walked out of view. There, lying down as one body in this circle of bodies, I felt the sense of feigned equality drawing out of my veins. The lie I had told to gain entrance into this clique of righteousness gave way. Though it seemed morally sound to begin with (a lie told to subvert the rules set against me; a lie that might, after all, save a life), suddenly, I would rather someone had died than that they have my blood under such conditions. Now, nothing was sacred. Not even these nurses – these smiling women; mothers and aunts and friends. All of a sudden they were hostile, everything was hostile. Gradually, all these emblems of safety, of comfort, were inverted. My blood was full of ghosts and I could hear them chanting in the rhythms of the room. Eventually, the nurse came over and removed the needle from my arm and put a plaster over the small wound. When I stood up, my vision clouded over with white shapes and bright, expanding circles. I fell to the floor with a smack and woke up in another world.

Since then I have taken that haunted blood and trod with it heavy in my body. When I walked down to the cemetery that January evening, a decade or more later, I was still walking into that other world. A counter-world, a place I had discovered that existed alongside the world I grew up in, but which was contrary, nocturnal, sacrosanct. It's hard to explain the thrill I first felt in discovering that, at night, along the streets and playing fields I grew up in, there were men like me, meeting in secret. Here was an alternative map, a film negative of the once familiar streets, a subversion of everything that had pushed me out. I spent teenage nights sneaking out of the house, pushing myself further towards those men – testing myself, my bravery, my capacity to be contrary. But that January night, after all the events of the intervening years, going down into the shadow of the great cathedral felt different. It was no longer bravery that compelled me, but disregard. At the lowest ebb of myself, what else could hurt me now?

Still, I was looking for something. Part of the attraction of the night-time was its intimacy. The only things awake were the animals, the blank-faced moon or, behind my house, the waterfowl crying out softly, the coots burbling and then slumping like stray boules into the black silk of the lake. In a perfect night – out of the city, or in a park somewhere away from the street lamps – I could almost float in it. The blackness covering me, hiding my body from itself, taking me in its arms, I imagined, as pure soul. That encompassing darkness, its gentle love, was what I needed. I swam in it. I wandered for miles around the city, urging myself each night to walk further and further into the dark spaces of the parks, to sit beside the streams I could barely see, to listen to the night-creatures, all my senses heightened in a state of alertness that was close to an erotic charge. Now, in the dulled synapses of my brain, only this brief danger seemed like living. I was trying to recover that teenage feeling I had lost. I would sit there, on a bench, on a rock, on a low-slung branch, and breathe the cold air into my lungs in deep, replenishing drags, then exhale, watching my white breath unfurl and dissipate in the silver light.

For weeks after I met the kickboxer in the cemetery gardens, I would walk down there at night, tentatively at first, afraid, but then bolder, with nothing to lose, hoping to find that exiled version of myself. I sensed my way down the path and between the gravestones and the statuary. Once, I mistook a statue of a woman weeping over a tomb for an actual woman. I bolted and slipped on the wet paving. Other times I would sit by the running stream, playing my fingers through its crystal chain until each ached with the cold. I warmed them in my mouth, tasting the clean, iron water. One evening I saw a couple come down to the spring and light a church candle, which they placed into a nook in the sandstone wall. The next day the spill of white wax had solidified and the guttering soot of the burning wick had marked the deep red of the rock. I ran my fingers over it and wondered if they had been praying, and what for. I found a gravestone of a woman called 'Moon', who died in 1888. I imagined her wide, bright face. I wandered amongst the strange, antique stonework – a pyramid, an urn, an angel whose head had been broken off, perhaps by the weather, perhaps by kids clambering over the graves. In one marble slab I found the shapes of shells and of fishbones. There were animal skeletons in the limestone. The strata of the shale, even at night, showed blue and then brown as it extended up towards the street above. I heard that John Newton, the former slave-ship captain who wrote the hymn 'Amazing Grace', surveyed the tides near here. I sang it in whispers under the rushing of the leaves, and thought of shackles and conversion and inadequacy.

Occasionally, I would hope to see the shape of the man I met here, walking along the winding path, pausing to light his cigarette, but I never did. After an hour or so I would take the steep far passage out by the cathedral entrance, hurrying through the grave-lined stone tunnel, always with the sense that someone was behind me, the prickling fear that someone would grab the collar of my jacket and drag me back down before I reached the orange glow of the street ahead. On the last evening I ever came here, before I joined Duke Street and started the long walk home past the Georgian terraces, I paused before the tall iron gates of the Oratory, gazing at its bright red door, the little rectangle of leaded glass above it, and pictured all the white statues standing in pin-drop silence inside. Perhaps, through the skylight, the stars and the moon were touching the alabaster and marble and making ripples of shadow over the sculpted bodies and the neat inscriptions. I could see the figure of a father, caught in perpetual mourning; the lone child playing its silent lute. 'Heard melodies are sweet, but those unheard / Are sweeter.' And what of them?

I thought of Jack, Elias, all the others who had entered the darkness and had struggled to leave it. I cannot speak for the unheard sounds of those in the graves below. But for the man I met – for all of them – for that endlessly linking river, with all its nodes and tributaries, I can offer whatever of it my body still holds. In my mind, on my lips, in my heart. I stood in the darkness, under the long shadow of the cathedral, and lifted my thumb up to my forehead, my mouth, my chest, and left a bright stain of blood on each.

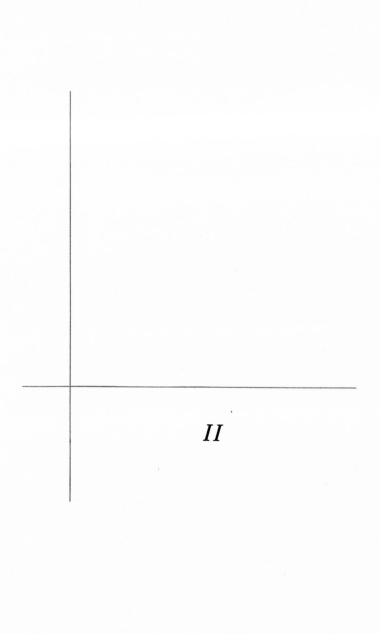

II

In the only photograph I have of Jack he is standing in the college's main courtyard, smiling straight back at me. An honest-to-god movie-star smile. Dimples, perfect white teeth, his thick brows, and his eyes glinting even at this distance, on this expired film. In real life his face could be gaunt, but on camera his bones caught the light and gave him this air of timelessness. His brown hair was dart-straight, so that it lifted in spikes even when he combed it and pushed it over to one side. His bowtie, in the picture, is slightly skewed, probably from where I'd been holding him, kissing his neck. He's in a black tuxedo, standing in front of a dodgem circuit, and there's the helter-skelter in the background I remember us going down. I can still feel his strong legs wrapped around my waist as we sat on the hessian sack, drunk, his hands quickly grasping mine as we pushed off from the platform on to the metal slide and pelted and spiralled towards the ground, tumbling out at the bottom in a heap of laughter.

Even though the photograph was taken only seven or eight years ago, the whole image feels like something from another time. It was before I met Elias, before I moved to Sweden, before everything changed. Jack and I had a brief relationship when I was at university. It was nothing fixed or regular, but he stayed in my mind as a sort of ideal, the prototype of everyone who came after. I always thought, somehow, that I'd see him again and that nothing would be different, that maybe we'd pick up right where we left off. Then, walking past the blossoming cherries in one of Liverpool's parks one Easter Sunday, I heard his voice in my head, singing a setting from Housman. When I got home, I looked him up online, expecting, as usual, for my search to come up with hardly any returns. A man with the same name in Massachusetts; someone whose date of birth was logged in a Parish register from Co. Kerry in 1847. Not my Jack. He was sceptical of the internet – didn't leave any trace online, wanted to be 'off the grid', and always put up a fight if I wanted to post a photo of him.

This particular photograph, too, came about in a way that strikes me, now I've left the college, as bizarrely old-fashioned. One day, during my second year at university, an email came through on the weekly round-up and we were told that a retired Fellow had donated a monthly sum to restart the college's Photography Society, and was looking for someone willing to take charge of the reboot. I agreed to handle it, which mainly involved keeping the darkroom stocked and throwing supplies out when they expired. I spent the first day in my new role sticking up cardboard around the door of the small room, so that the darkness might be absolute. I had almost no idea what I was doing. I ordered the chemicals over the phone from Jessops and picked up the white, sloshing Ilford canisters in the shop in town, then cycled them back up to college in my basket. Often, they went out of date before they were used. But I loved to go down into that basement darkroom under Commons, where there were no windows, just that rusty iron door that led back up to the courtyard. The only thing down there, except for the exposing trays and the enlarger, was an old Casio radio and cassette player, and the only cassette was a late-80s Philips recording of Holst's *Planet Suite*.

There was something so camply dramatic about the opening military bars of 'Mars, The Bringer of War' filling the small, brick-walled room as I set to work. I remember feeling cinematic, bathed in the low, red light as I poured out the stop bath and the fix, carefully unravelling my film and turning on the enlarger to see the small boxes of the negatives projected, adjusting the aperture ring until the bright image lit up in focus on the baseboard. Then, with the light flicked off, I'd move the paper on to the plate underneath the enlarger, and when I had it right, turn the light back on with a burst, photo'ing the image on to the sensitive white surface, invisibly marking it. Sometimes I'd get the chemicals in the trays mixed up, forgetting which was which, and have to start over again. Or I'd get too distracted by the music and have to turn it off to concentrate. I had an old Nikon, which I bought because my father had the same camera, and I always loved his early family portraits: the texture of the matte photo paper, the depth of the image behind the sitters as the foliage of the garden blurred into a deep summer haze.

I was wrapped up in the slowness of it, the alchemy. Occasionally, the film in the Nikon slipped, so I had a few rolls of double-exposed photographs where winter landscapes sat like lace over the faces of friends, and suddenly a dinner in the dining room was accompanied by snow-laden firs and apple boughs shook with hoar frost. But this photo of Jack came out crisp and defined. I took it in black and white, and it gave him a timelessness, a sort of classic ease that seemed out of place in the twenty-first century. I remember thinking, the first time I saw it taking shape in the developing solution, that it was like uncovering an artefact: taking the plastic tray in both hands and gently rocking the solution over the floating paper, until it sank and was covered, and eventually the more exposed outlines of the image began to appear, emerging out of nowhere. First, the darker background on the white sheet, the far places of the quad where the flash of the camera didn't strike anything. Then, the image of Jack's suit, the shape of his body, the dark of his hair and his eyebrows; the hundred little lightbulbs on the tower of the helter-skelter; a food stall; a waiter serving drinks; blurred figures caught smashing their dodgem cars into each other, the electricity sparking on the gauze roof. And then there he was, like a ghost, smiling at me from under the clear solution. I picked the paper up out of the tray and let it drip dry, shaking it a little, then moved it into the stop bath, rocking it again briefly, and then once more into the fix, before I took it out, slick with the fluids, and hung it up with wooden clips on the drying line.

So, although I hadn't spoken to him for a year or more, and had few physical things to remember him by, I still heard his voice when I saw the bobbing white flowers of the cherry trees in the park that Easter. I sat down, casually, while I was alone in the apartment, and typed Jack's name into the search engine, expecting the usual list of misdirections and red herrings, but this time the first result was a funeral notice, his name, his town, sadly missed, his sorrowful parents and sisters, and I just stared in disbelief, checking it, reading it over and over to find some mistake, some sign that this wasn't my Jack, but someone else's. And then, right there, his photograph, his broad smile beaming out against some alpine background, the hyphen from his year of birth completed, closed off. Last August, his body was taken from his parents' house to a chapel in Glencoe, the Scottish village where he'd grown up, and he'd had a quiet service, only family, and I hadn't even known. I stared into the blue light of the computer, in total silence, and didn't even cry, because I didn't believe it was real. If he'd died, I thought, surely I'd have felt some shift in the world, or sensed some thread of my own life snipped and unravelling inside me. A rupture in the matrix of time – some past completed, some possible future shut off. But nothing. He had gone and I hadn't known a thing, and had carried on as normal, all those months, hearing his voice, as if he were speaking from wherever he was, as if it were still echoing from its source, and he was still there, still someone I might return to.

And because I couldn't find anything more of him online, I pulled out the drawer under my bed and searched and searched through all the old albums until I found his photograph. He had come to the Spring Ball alone, and, looking back, that would mean it was a few months after the first time we'd met. I was wandering, drunk, looking for the friends I'd lost, when I saw him standing by himself in the main quad. He had his back to me, but when he turned around I caught his eye and he smiled and I walked over to him, looking down at the floor, scared to hold his gaze. He was so handsome. You could see the muscular set of his body even through his suit. He always stood with a straight back, seemed poised and aware of his own movements, but not in a repressed or awkward way. It was as though he had perfected the art of himself. He was careful and attentive to what his body might do for him. In other words, he was conscious of his own desirability – flirted with it and gave it freely. A rare thing, really, in a young gay man – to be so confident and shameless in the pleasures of the body. He was older than me and I always felt a few steps behind him, always catching up to the level of his freedom.

His voice was deep and was set with a rich Highland undertow that swept along beneath the words, running them into one another, something I took a while to tune in to. I hardly remember now what we said to each other that night at the ball. Mostly, it was a rush of kissing, holding on to each other, his arm slung over my shoulder, mine (somewhat daringly, I thought) around his lower back. We spent hours drinking and dancing and then kissing again, no one important except for us two, the whole background of the night blurred out of focus. I could hardly bear to leave him alone, even for a minute, was drawn to him with an eagerness that was a sort of disbelief. We went to the bathroom together, and kissed for so long in the cubicle that by the time we stumbled out, a line of people had formed. I must have gone bright red, but he took my hand and laughed loudly and ran off with me down the corridor. He was always laughing at my shyness. He didn't believe in it himself – he was so headstrong, always against the grain, and made me feel silly and old-fashioned for being embarrassed at all. Part way through the night, dancing in a hot, strobe-lit tent in the old courtyard, he pulled me close to him and slipped a tablet into my hand, then took his pint and swallowed his pill, and I did the same – the first time I'd ever done it – and the pulse of my body sank and then quickened into a rhythmic state of euphoria, my cheeks tired with smiling and the muscles moving in my body, and Jack was the only person in the world.

That photograph is at the back of an old album now, amongst others from the same night. There are a few of my brothers, who had come down to Cambridge for the occasion, and spent the evening marvelling at and mocking the pretence of it all in equal measure. There are the faces of a few friends I have fallen out of touch with, some I can't even remember the names of any more. We all stayed up until sunrise, when the April light spread over the large grounds of the college, setting the main tower aglow and leaving the courtyards already like a sham of their earlier glamour. Jack and I had been together all night, and I'd hardly seen the others and felt guilty for leaving them, but I found them standing under the main tower-arch of the building, trying to call me on their phones, and I walked up to them with Jack alongside me.

In that final year I had been given a large 'set' – a bedroom with a sofa, bookcases and a living area – right in the apex of the college's old wing, overlooking the main court. I led everyone upstairs and they slept on my bedroom floor. Suits discarded over the backs of armchairs; white dress shirts crumpled up on the carpet. It was 4 a.m., but I didn't want the night to be over. I couldn't bear to let sleep eclipse the perfect drunkenness and the taste of Jack and the feeling of his body, warm against mine, his hands pulling me into him, stumbling into another kiss. When the others had started to settle, I heard him rustling slightly, and then whispering my name, urgently, conspiratorially, winking and gesturing to the door. I pulled on my trousers again, grabbed my jacket, and slowly and quietly twisting the handle of the lock, and let myself out into the now sunlit corridor. The college was deadly quiet, but the birds were starting up outside, roused and awake. After a moment, the door handle turned again, slowly, and Jack slipped out, still putting on his dress shoes, grinning at me like a schoolboy.

At the far end of the corridor, there was a small turret, a

decorative addition to the neo-Gothic, nineteenth-century building. I nodded towards it, and we both snuck off through the low door and into the spiral staircase, where I had to lean backwards to keep my head from skimming the brick ceiling as it sloped. At the bottom, we unlatched the door and stepped out into the cold, dewy morning, our bodies still buzzing slightly with the wine and the pills, a slow, hazy ease, tired but peaceful. The cedars on the striped lawn were dazzling, their great boughs shook full of water and the darkest shade of green. All the red brick of the college was warming, and there was no one around, as though the whole place was brand new. He pulled me close to him from behind, then turned me so my back was against the closed door, and lifted me up against it, talking to me closely, smiling. I could feel the strength of him then – hardly straining at all as he held me up, and I felt light.

We walked along the outside of the wing, where the formal gardens were full of white hyacinths and the scent of viburnums was lilting headily over the lawns. At the far end of the grounds there was an orchard of plum and apple and pear trees, some of them as old as the college itself. In the first month of autumn the ground was nearly untreadable, strewn over with the mulch of rotten fruit and humming with wasps and bees, but now the grass was soft, shooting with new blades, and the heat of an unusually warm month had brought the buds to bursting early. We lifted the metal latch of the gate and I waited for Jack to walk ahead, then closed it with a hollow clank behind us. He ambled off into the middle of the orchard, away from the path and into the longer grass, and lay down, full of confidence, before he realised how much dew was soaking through his trousers. He jumped up, swearing quietly, then turned to see me laughing, and undid his fly to show me the dark watermark on his boxers, spread into a sort of butterfly over his buttocks.

'See!' he said, and I slapped them, lightly, the wet fabric clinging to his skin; and when I kissed him, I couldn't stop kissing him, and I felt him getting hard against me.

'Up here,' I said, pointing to one of the low branches of the apple tree behind us, and I clambered up, scuffing my dress shoes against the bark, but not caring. By the time I was sitting on the branch I had green marks and bark stains on my trousers, and tried to brush them off. Jack followed, annoyingly swift and easy in his climbing, lifting himself up with one effortless pull. I felt the branch sink as he shimmied on to it, and knew the weight of his body, and ached to feel it on me, the lowering of the tree gently suggesting the heft of his muscles. I held on to the branch with both hands, as though it were a conduit between us, and I felt its give as though it were me, and not the tree, who was sighing under him.

We sat in quiet next to each other, and I knew he was happy to be there. He stroked his hand up and down my thigh. The scene was peaceful and calm, but I was acutely aware of his movements. For all the birds and the sun and the blossoms, all I could think of was his hand, touching my leg, its sliding up and down, wondering how high it might go, and feeling an involuntary shudder as his grip loosened and strengthened slightly. After a while, he looked at me, half-joking: 'Do you want to suck my dick?'

I pushed him in the arm and told him to fuck off, grinning, and I lay my head between his shoulder and his neck, smelling the faint scent of his aftershave on his skin. He moved his head slowly from one side to the other, rubbing his stubble gently against my cheek. I'd always been guarded when it came to my own desires. Perhaps it was some latent

shame, or a longing, as someone who had spent years setting myself apart through books and cleverness, not to be
reduced to my body, which was a thing everyone had, and
something I wanted to distinguish myself from. 'Soon,' I
said, smiling at him, and he just said 'Sure', in that way that
Scottish people say 'sure' to mean 'sure', and not in the
English way that always feels inflected with doubt.

After a while, out of nowhere, and quite out of character,
Jack started humming a tune, and smirked at me as though he
were mocking the idyllic trap I'd set. Then, he broke out into
a joking English baritone, a setting of a Housman poem,
'Loveliest of trees, the cherry now', barely making it through
the lines without laughing, trilling the *r*'s and drawing out the
vowels to absurd lengths. He knew the whole song, even the
middle verse that always tripped me up with its talk of scores
and springs, its poetic calculation of how many years the
singer has left to live. But as he went on, he lost the mockery,
and sank into a sweet, almost earnest singing, his own accent
coming through, so the words weren't those of an English
countryman any more, but of Jack, no longer sitting ironi-
cally against the scene, but inflecting it with his own voice. I
can still hear him now. In fact, I can never hear the song any
more without hearing him singing it.

> And since to look at things in bloom
> Fifty springs are little room,
> About the woodlands I will go
> To see the cherry hung with snow.

Jack's voice, joining the spring morning in the orchard, a
little song of pleasure and grief so intertwined it would
break your heart to hear it. After a while, he started to

whistle the song instead, and the birds were singing, too – a different tune, but no less steeped in a happiness brought on by the sunshine and the moving of the year. And I sat and listened, my head on his shoulder, and whatever it was the birds knew, my heart also sang.

*

On the day I found out that Jack had died, it seemed as though a part of my life, a part that had been suspended in my subconscious, suddenly locked into place. For me, his death began to seem part of a lineage: all these men I knew and walked beside, collapsing under the pressured atmosphere of the world. And I looked to myself and began to see my life differently, as though all the things I had thought or done as I grew up took a new perspective and crystallised. That day, I felt as if we were all walking headlong into some winnowing fire, and the further we walked, the less of ourselves we seemed able to carry with us.

All that afternoon I sat in my room and thought of Jack. I looked for any physical traces I might still have of him, but found only that one photograph. After too long spent staring into the unfocused space between my bookshelf and the far wall of my bedroom, I had lost the sound of his singing. But then, new words seemed to surface and I saw Jack again, walking ahead of me. It was a poem by Gerard Manley Hopkins that I had in my mind, but I could remember only the first line: 'Sometimes a lantern moves along the night.' Perhaps there was an answer in it, some clue, some remnant of Jack that my subconscious was pushing forward. I went to the bookshelf and took down my old, worn copy of the poems. The spine was broken, and the first section of the book had come loose. There was foxing on the pages – brown circles and specks, probably from the damp wall of my room. Hopkins was a Jesuit priest, a Victorian, and for years I'd read his poems and his diaries and heard him speaking to me. I felt a kinship and an understanding with him. In my mind I had made him into a sort of guardian. He loved other men, too, but could never say it, though his poems are full of their bodies, their beauty. Nature, for him, was the presence of God incarnating through the world, and he invented a word – *inscape* – to mean uniqueness, the quality that makes each thing in the world a constant expression of its own self, and nothing else. He tried to pinpoint the inscapes of waves, clouds, bluebells, hawks. I took that word to be a sort of paradigm of utopia, especially for Hopkins, a man who was wracked by the chaos of being himself, of knowing what his self might be.

I found the poem, 'The Lantern out of Doors', and read it, wondering what it was I remembered, what Hopkins was trying to tell me. 'Men go by me,' he wrote,

> whom either beauty bright
> In mould or mind or what not else makes rare:
> They rain against our much-thick and marsh air
> Rich beams, till death or distance buys them quite.

I saw Jack and the others walking away from me, all those rich beams thrown through the air, and one by one they were going out. I read it again. There was so much I couldn't know from the poem. Who were the men and where were they going? I supposed that for Hopkins the answer was probably to heaven or to Christ, but neither of those things meant much to me any more.

Those lines ran through my head that day, the men walking in the darkness, glowing like lanterns in the gloom of the world. They caught something of my sense of the sad inevitability of Jack's death, gave it a history and a movement. But the lines, unintentionally or not, also made me aware of something unchanging, a tradition that should have ended long ago. There was a haunting music underscoring them. In Hopkins's time, though I couldn't be sure that he was writing about men like him and like me, the regime against what he knew as 'sin' or 'deviance' or 'inversion' was much more apparent, much more obvious. As a priest, Hopkins knew this intimately. For him, everything was hidden, everything kept down. And, though so much is different now – over a century since Hopkins died, a young priest on a placement in Dublin – still there was this procession of men, walking beside me, people I knew and loved being added to it, and, one by one, their lights were being put out. In their midst, I felt my own light flickering, too.

Later that night, unable to sleep, I sat up at my desk, still trying to find traces of Jack online. A photo I hadn't seen before, something he'd written, a video perhaps, but there was nothing but the funeral notice. I didn't know how he had died, but I had a sense of it. My mind rushed through images of him, then images of my ex-boyfriend Elias, then all the other boys I had known and lost, their faces appearing and then falling back into the crowd. They all had something in common, but I hadn't made the connection until now, and the connection brought things into focus, made things feel more real, set up a chain of threat and consequence in my mind. It felt dangerous to admit it, as though the commonality was a sort of curse, a brokenness in them, in us, but I knew the brokenness was in the world instead.

I remembered, then, a neighbour from when I was young – a kind, large woman who sometimes used to care for my brothers and me when my parents were at work – telling me that I shouldn't be gay. I was perhaps only six or seven at the time, but she knew. I knew it, too. It was as if she had peered into the deep, secret part of my soul and seen what I was hiding. I flushed crimson and went quiet. I felt as if I were being told off, as if I had done something wrong, but I didn't know what I had done, and I didn't know how to change it. It was fashionable, she said, sneeringly, but gay people weren't happy. She said she didn't want me to be unhappy like them. I had known this secret thing about myself for as long as I could remember, and spent many nights, tucked up with my night light spinning stars across the ceiling of my room, wondering if I could escape this hurtling into disaster. If I hid it forever, perhaps I would never be found out. If I admitted it – or if, worst of all, it got out without my control – I knew that everything after that point would fall into an abyss: my family, my safety, my life. There, again – that dangerous sense of inevitability.

I suppose she thought she was protecting me. I can recall this conversation, along the same lines, with many people throughout my childhood and youth. People seemed to have an uncanny knack for warning me about something I thought they couldn't see. When anything gay was mentioned – in the newspaper or on TV – I would sink into my chair and try to pass through the moment invisibly. I could feel their eyes watching me. Sometimes, people would make sounds of disgust when they saw men holding hands, and I knew – with that acute childhood intuition – that it was me they were disgusted by. Perhaps they didn't know it was me, but I knew it, and that was enough. Every word, every gesture, every implicit warning, each was another nail I used to seal up the little box in which I kept that secret part of myself hidden. The more I heard, the more I saw, the more certain it became that I could never open that box.

When they said, 'I'm just scared that you'll be unhappy,' what I really felt they were saying was 'I am scared that if you continue being yourself, we will make you unhappy.' A sort of threat, veiled as a kindness. Perhaps they told themselves that they wanted to protect me from being unhappy. After all, how hard is it to keep a secret, if the prize for keeping it is a life of happiness? But I'm sure they also wanted to protect themselves from their association with me, and the violence that might come with it. They did not want me to be happy by making happiness possible, but by asking me to live in a world which they knew was set against me. Their critique was of me, not of themselves. They said, 'I am scared you will be unhappy.' They meant, 'It is better to be on the right-hand side of the devil than in his path.' And so there was an admission, something in them that knew they were complicit.

I didn't know how to make sense of it, all this loss, this brokenness. How could I know what had taken Jack and all those others? Would it take me, too? In Hopkins's poem there is a disembodied light, though we imagine someone to be carrying it. I thought of it again, and of going after that light. 'Sometimes,' Hopkins wrote, 'a lantern moves along the night. / That interests our eyes. And who goes there?' Where are they coming from and where are they going? 'Where from and bound, I wonder, where, / With, all down darkness wide, his wading light?' That disembodied figure, moving through the night, holding up the yellow-angled beams of a lantern. I decided to follow that ghost, back through my own life, through the lives I had known and lost, through the lives I had not known, but wished to know; to skirt the darkness, to walk behind the swinging light, to get to the heart of where it was taking me, which is where, after all, I had come from.

*

In the October of my second Michaelmas term as an under-graduate, six months or so before I had taken that photograph of Jack at the ball, I unlocked my bike from the sheds at the end of the college drive and cycled into the lowering dusk, down Castle Hill and into the centre of Cambridge. My basket juddered along the cobblestones as I went past the colleges of St John's and Trinity towards King's Parade, where the King's Chapel stood imposingly, backlit by a red, autumnal sunset and blocked from view only by the crisp-edged leaves of the horse chestnut by the Senate House. It was a Thursday, which meant it was the one night of the week when a small pub down an alley off Bene't Street turned, surprisingly, into a tiny haven of dancing. Not the usual Cambridge student night, which, as far as I could tell, meant drunk private-schooled boys downing beers and beating their chests, and drunk private-schooled girls hoping to marry them. Here, for one night a week, all the queers of the city came out of their college rooms and out of the suburbs, and met, often awkwardly, in the downstairs room of an old public house. Disco tunes, remixes of pop music done over with heavy beats. Nothing glamorous about it. The choice of drinks comprised a few lagers, gins and vodka, and there was barely enough room to stand without also finding yourself unwit-tingly in the queue for the bar. Here, though, outside of the claustrophobic privilege of the university, there were people I had at least one thing in common with.

I rattled my blue bike along the alley, lifting off and standing up on one pedal, like a postman, until I pulled to a stop by the church, where I ignored the penalty notice and locked my bike to the railings. I'd already had a few glasses of wine back in my college room, hoping to dull my anxiety, and when I walked along the passage to the pub, I could see all the windows already fogged up and hot with condensation, a warm glow of light inside. There were muffled noises, beats, and shadows moving about. It was still nothing like the cheap, rowdy bars I was used to in my northern home town, but it was something, and I was glad to have it.

That was the night I met Hasan, who led me to Jack. The hot downstairs room of the pub was small and filled with young people trying out their make-up and the outfits they wouldn't get away with in the normal Cambridge bars. I stood by the wall, warm pint in hand, and I wanted to join them – I have always wanted to join them – in dressing up. Skirts and glitter and sequins and harnesses, but then, as now, something held me back. As a minor concession, I used to wear a golden cross earring on my left ear. It hung from the bottom of a gold hoop, which I'd had since I was sixteen, when I had snuck out into town with a friend into the upstairs room of a shop that sold cannabis paraphernalia and poppers and healing crystals. I remember being embarrassed when a boy at school pointed at it, laughing, saying I had got 'the gay ear' (my left one) pierced, but there was a glow of pride under the shame I felt, a pride that I had been brave enough to mark myself out. Still, I always felt myself to be looking in on an ideal queerness. Only the occasional pill, or too much wine, could help me step over that invisible line towards the others.

I drank my pint and ordered another. Every so often, I would walk around the pub as if I was searching for a friend.

I didn't want to look as though I was there alone. But, after a half hour or so, the dance floor filled up and I felt less conspicuous. I eased my way into the crowd. Before long I was dancing, or swaying, up by the DJ booth, facing the decks and turning around occasionally to see who was there, hoping to spot a familiar face; and then there he was, Hasan, right beside me. He was much shorter than I was. I hardly noticed him at first, but when I looked down I saw his bright face, his strong jaw, and deep-set brown eyes that kept on catching mine, then looking away, as if it were all an accident. He was French, a gymnast, it turned out, though he'd come to Cambridge to study History of Art, the sort of subject I hadn't known existed until I got here.

I think he'd been working his way towards me in the crowd. He pushed through right next to me, and after a while I felt his arm against mine, then his hand, and he started dancing against me and I against him. After a few songs, he tried to speak to me, and I leant down to him, but the music was loud and I couldn't make out what he was saying. Eventually, he gestured to me to follow him and we went upstairs and out into the street for a cigarette. Out of the blue, but casually enough, he told me I should come home with him to meet his boyfriend. His name was Jack and he was 'up working late'. Hasan offered the words with a sort of innocence, a secret code for what he actually meant. I was drunk enough by this point that I said 'OK,' but I said the word as if I were only agreeing to what was made explicit, and was unaware of the thrill of fear and excitement implied by the subtext. We placed our glasses on a bench outside the pub and walked off down the alley.

I unlocked my bike from the church railings and wheeled it alongside us as we walked back down King's Parade, and

Hasan told me about himself. He was gentle and slightly feminine, and he walked like a boy I used to fancy in high school – arms lifted out by his side, as though the muscles wouldn't let them sit straight along his torso. He had close-cropped, curly black hair, and looked up to me all the time as though I might protect him from something. As we passed along the wall of Caius, I suddenly felt out of my depth.

'Actually, sorry, I think . . .'

He just smiled at me, and carried on talking.

'Lock your bike up here,' he said, pointing to the lamp-post at the edge of the cobbled street. 'It's easier than trying to take it into college.'

I took out my chain from the basket and looped it around the back wheel, twisting the key in the padlock and letting the chain fall with a chime against the metal post.

He led me down the path past the porter's lodge, where an old man was sitting, reading under the light of a small lamp. We both instinctively kept our heads down, talking casually – an old after-hours trick when entering a college that wasn't yours – hoping they wouldn't ask us whether we lived there or not, or what we were doing. When we were out of sight, we stepped right through into the Great Court, which was empty except for a girl sitting on a step over by the south side, smoking a cigarette. It burned orange and then faded again into the dark as she lifted her head and shook her hair to one side, blowing out a quick funnel of white smoke which dissipated into the air above her. The gravel crunched under our feet as we walked down the centre of the crossways path towards the fountain. It was a clear, quiet night, and only a few windows were still lit up with people working, but a low fog was already settling in the cold, close to the lawns, and there was a dampness in the air even though the sky was open and cloudless.

We passed the colonnade of the Wren Library, the pair of us just two shadows stretching and shrinking between the arches, and then came out at the back of the college into a less considered space, concreted over, where some cars were parked and large dustbins stood in rows along the boundary wall. Hasan, by this point, was a few paces ahead, too used to the surroundings to take much notice, and he turned back to me. I was staring up at the buildings and I felt him watching me for a while before he got impatient.

'Come on,' he said. 'It's freezing out here.'

I was wondering if I was ready to go with him, whether I was ready to take that one step further into the new life I was discovering away from home. Here, I was an adult, all the world of good and bad choices open before me. I looked over to him and assented, not with any gesture, but by turning towards him and following as he walked up to the arched wooden door and opened it, the sliver of yellow light expanding behind him. He stood there, silhouetted, waiting for me to catch up.

Upstairs, the door to Jack's room was unlocked, so we walked right in. There was a Brian Eno record playing, and a few church candles were guttering out by the latticed window. Jack, it turned out, was asleep in the bed – fully clothed, with just a rough-looking blanket curled around his leg, his hand tucked under the pillow beneath his head.

'I've brought someone to meet you,' Hasan whispered, though quite loudly, and he said my full name, as though I'd been expected, as though Jack would know who I was, though we'd never met.

Hasan didn't wait for Jack to wake up, and instead walked

over to the small alcove on the far side of the room, where
there were piles of books – editions of Attic drama, a bright
red hardback of Lucretius' *On the Nature of Things*, a few
worn-out grammars. They almost looked like they'd been
placed there as a prop to signal a studiousness at odds with
the rest of the room. I ran my eyes over the bright green
Loeb editions of Euripides, which were taken out of the
shelf and stacked in a random pile, and tried briefly to read
the words on a notepad that was scribbled over with black
biro. Under the bookshelves was a small white fridge, which
Hasan opened with a clunk. I looked up, embarrassed at my
own curiosity. Hasan took out some beers with screw tops,
handed one to me, and then walked back over to Jack, leaning close to him this time, shaking him gently awake and
whispering something to him.

Jack turned over and looked across the room, saw me and
smiled, saying a sleepy 'Hello' as he slowly pulled himself
up, so that he was sitting over the edge of the bed, rubbing
his eyes, his hair ruffled.

I said, 'Hey,' followed immediately by 'Sorry.' I didn't
know what I was apologising for.

There was a two-seater sofa by a small fireplace, in which
a few pinecones were propped up on top of each other, and
I sat down on it and took a sip of my beer. Jack got up off
the bed and came to sit next to me.

'I've been waiting for you, you know.'

I didn't know what he meant. I couldn't tell if he meant
tonight, or if he meant he'd been waiting for me for a long
time. I didn't know whether he meant he'd been waiting for
me personally, or if he meant he'd been waiting for someone
like me. All I knew, in that moment, was that I was happy
to be waited for. For the first time I felt what it was like to

be on the receiving end of reciprocated desire. Still, this wasn't without a sense of discomfort. To know that I had been expected, especially when for me this was all so unexpected, so impromptu, put me on edge. I had the uneasy sense, then, of my own passivity, my own susceptibility to coercion, and felt childish and out-of-depth.

Nevertheless, when he put his hand around the back of my head and brought me slowly towards him, I leant in and kissed him, closing my eyes before our lips touched. We had hardly said anything, but it didn't matter. I was feeling braver now. I put my beer down and reached my hand across on to his thigh, and after a few seconds he leant back and pulled off his T-shirt, lifting his arms up over his head, so the collar ruffled his hair upwards and he came out of it slightly flustered. I brushed his hair back and kissed him again, deeper this time, loosening into him. Buoyed by a sense of my own reflection in his gaze, I seemed to inhabit myself differently, and I took off my own shirt, too. At this point I remembered Hasan. It was strange to have forgotten him, but I had, and I pulled back from Jack to look around the room, to check if Hasan was OK, to check if all of this was OK, but I saw that he was just sitting on the bed, drinking his beer, watching us, but also looking out of the window occasionally, as though we were perhaps interesting, but nothing outside the realm of the ordinary.

As I was lying there on the sofa, with my head in Jack's lap, he held the end of a half-smoked cigarette to my lips and I dragged it, coughing slightly. I blew the smoke up into the air away from his face. I could feel the hardness of him pressing gently into the base of my neck, and I looked up at him, altered by the strange angle, and he looked down at me and smiled slightly and took the cigarette in between his fingers and smoked it again, then tapped it against a glass ashtray on the bookcase. Every so often I felt the shape of his erection lift under my neck, then sink again, involuntarily, the blood moving through it. Jack carried on smoking and nodding his head rhythmically, and then slowly swaying it to the music, his legs spread open and me just looking up at him and at the ceiling, then taking another drag of his cigarette as he lowered the end of it towards my mouth and held it to my lips while I breathed it in.

As the beats of the music quickened, catching up with my pulse, he took another drag, and put the cigarette into the little groove of the ashtray. He took my head in his hands and leant forward over me and brought his lips to mine. Slowly, he opened his mouth so that the wreathes and tendrils of blue smoke bloomed out of him and over me, and he kissed me through them, keeping his lips apart so that the smoke passed into my mouth and back into his, warm and visible. Smoking – another broken taboo – became a sort of communion, an image of things passing out of his body and into mine, ephemeral, but also present. Kissing Jack, I was aware of a constant, suspended pleasure – the touch of his lips on mine, the occasional soft bite of my lip, his tongue. It was his way of keeping desire, of holding it at a pitch, in abeyance, without ever satisfying it. The smoke was like pleasure – something we could taste and feel the heat of, but never quite touch.

When I opened my eyes again, Hasan was standing over me, too, and he put his hand in mine, pushing each of his fingers between my own. I lifted myself up, and when he took off his shirt I saw the long muscles of his back and followed them down to the blue horizontal of his underwear. He took my head towards him and tilted it to one side, gently scratching my neck with his stubble, kissing it, and then journeying upwards, where he took my earlobe in his mouth and played with the gold cross earring, tugging it softly with his teeth, taking it just to the edge of pain before letting it go. For hours, then, the three of us moved together, interlocking, a sort of trinity, loosening and tightening, as though between us we might dissolve the boundaries of the self.

*

A few weeks went by and I didn't hear from either Hasan or Jack, so a shame set in, along with a conviction that I must have been a disappointment, and the whole scene began to be recast in a less glowing hue. At hall one evening, over some lukewarm wine and bad dessert, my friends (who I hadn't told about that night) were gossiping, and said that another boy from college had gone up to the same room, and done the same thing, so what had attained for me a sort of pivotal significance was quickly recalibrated as just an unremarkable event in other people's lives. It was just like me, I thought, to attach this weight and meaning to something ordinary, to raise it to the level of some higher experience, and I was embarrassed that I had thought that it had meant the same to Hasan and Jack, too. Even then, I suppose, I was a poet, already in the irritating habit of turning life into metaphor, with all the added self-grandeur of a postponed adolescence.

Nevertheless, something inside me had changed; a bravery of sorts had broken through, and I began to learn that pushing the bounds of my morality, or of convention, was not only possible, but something I might need to do, repeatedly, as I made my way into a new life with men. I had so much of the world to cast off if I was ever going to be free.

At the same pub, on a different night not long afterwards, I met another man – older, this time, though still in his late twenties. An Austrian PhD student, who was taller than me and had a bulk to him that wasn't possible for younger men. I loved the close-cropped blonde hair on his chest, his accent that combined the long vowels of English RP with a distinctly German intonation. We had nothing in common, really, except that I was in awe of him and he knew it. One afternoon he asked me to come over to his house for a drink and we had green tea in his kitchen, where an unshaded bulb hung and flickered sometimes above a Formica table. I knew, of course, that I hadn't come over for tea, but he held the pretence for a while, and then offered to show me his room. He had a single bed, which would have been too small for even an average sized person, never mind this burly six-foot-six man. I sat on the edge of it as he talked, and when he came to sit beside me he took the cup out of my hand and placed it on the window ledge, which meant that something was about to happen.

He put his hand around my throat and pushed me back on to the bed, and climbed on top of me and kissed me, which was the sort of thing I'd fantasised about – this power of men, this being overpowered – but the reality of it unnerved me. His thumb pressed hard into my neck, his grip around me, the weight of his body: it was all I could think about when he kissed me. At some point I realised that I couldn't have got out from under him if I wanted to, and I started to panic and to push against him. His response was to bite down on my lip, and I flinched and pushed back harder this time. I could taste the sweet, iron taste of blood in my mouth, and his eyes had a sort of intensity to them, and, before I knew it, I was saying, 'Get the fuck off me!

Get the fuck off me!' and pushing against his shoulders. Eventually, he did. He looked confused. I didn't know if I'd overreacted, if this was normal. What was I doing here anyway, if not to ask for what he was giving me? He said sorry and tried to kiss me again, but I stood up, pulling my clothes on quickly, and said I had to leave. I stepped out of the house into the mid-afternoon drizzle and cycled home in a daze, my neck tender, my bottom lip sore.

I met him again, anyway, a few days later. After I had cooled off, I began to think of the danger of him. I wanted to be wanted like that again. I tried to see the coercion, the imbalance of power and strength, but then I knew I had driven it with my longing. Perhaps my fear of him was also a fear of myself, a form of shame at wanting him, and I had punished him for my own desire. Still, when it came down to it, I was too anxious to go back up to his room. When, inevitably, my eye was caught by someone else, I stopped replying to his texts. Once, when I was walking through town after a night out with some friends, he drove past me and shouted 'Slut!' out of the rolled-down window of his car. I turned to my friends and baulked in embarrassment and pretended not to know who he was.

These stoppings and startings, these gradual assays into sex, were often lonely and unshared, and seemed every time to be more daring, pushing me outside the bounds of what my straight peers were doing, or not doing, and I only learnt later that this was a feeling shared by many queer people – a sense of lonely discovery, followed by the light of community. Later that term, over coffee in a tea room on Mill Road, I met up with Hasan, who had begun texting me, off and on, sometimes flirting, sometimes not. We didn't really mention Jack, except that Hasan told me he was doing well with his research and was changing the topic of his thesis, something about Heraclitus' cosmic fragments.

I asked about Hasan's life and he told me about coming to Cambridge and how he had felt a sense of escape. He could be someone else here. He could be many different people if he wanted to be. The pretence of the place was, not surprisingly, conducive to pretending. Over his cup of coffee he told me that his grandfather, who raised him, had used to make him eat orange rinds as a punishment. Hasan would peel off the skin and hand each segment of fruit to his grandfather, who would keep them in a blue patterned bowl on the kitchen counter. When all that was left in Hasan's hand was the husk and the rind, he'd put the whole lot into his mouth quickly and chew and close his eyes and swallow the bitter skin as fast as he could. The theory, according to his grandfather, was that it would toughen him up, would make him less susceptible to the effeminacy he showed in childhood. Now Hasan had a sort of ritual. Whenever he ate oranges, he would keep the rind and burn it in the fireplace in his college room. He told me that he loved the citrus-smoke and the fizzle it made as the acid sparked in the hearth.

*

I never got as close to Jack as I wanted to. He was always busy with his PhD, something I had only a vague notion of. I didn't know what he did with his days and he rarely answered my messages. He kept himself guarded, and seemed to let go into a flamboyance of hedonism and then shut down again, for months at a time, working away in his room, calling me late at night to talk about his family, who he seemed to struggle with, and sometimes he would be drunk on the other end of the phone, talking about the Church or repression, things that sounded like the typically undergraduate enthusiasms for rebellion, but in retrospect seemed to be Jack's way of working out the knot of himself, of trying to loosen his mind into freedom. One night he called me in such a fit of sobbing that I left college past midnight and cycled into town to meet him. I found him in the concreted square where the bins were. He was leaning against a pillar in a pair of torn jean shorts and a mesh top, barely able to stand. His eyeliner was smeared around his eyes and across the backs of his hands, which were freezing cold when I took them between mine, blowing on them to warm them up.

After we graduated, I saw him only a few times. For a while, he had a blog, and I saw photos of him sometimes, getting thinner and thinner, partying in Mykonos or Berlin. He said he was happy and I believed him. But, looking back after reading that funeral notice, I sensed something else in those memories, something I had missed the first time around. It was like a music I hadn't taken the time to tune my ear to. Now, though, after what had happened with Elias, I recognised it. With a haunting completion, those notes had played out, their minor undercurrent picked up and played into prominence. I knew that music now. Its strain seemed to run through the lives of so many of the men I knew – a sort of counterpoint, shimmering in the background, rising and falling from the melody. So, as a chord is struck and must be carried through, Jack's death tempered me. It rang through the pitch of my life, scoring it backwards, suddenly chiming every minor note into place and revealing a pattern of them, which I set out to follow and to make sense of.

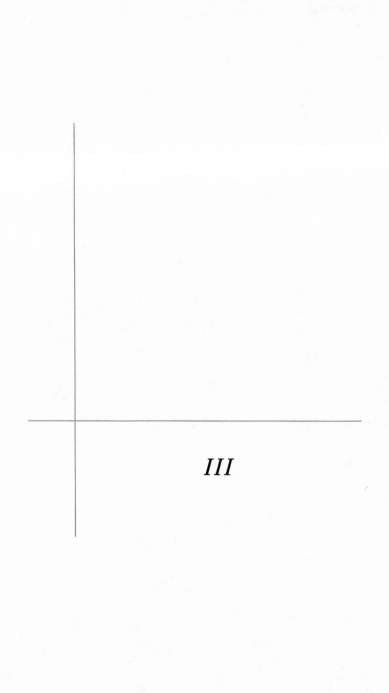

III

After graduation I took up an unpaid internship in publishing, using the last of my money to pay for food and staying on friends' sofas in London, but after three months it came to nothing and I was broke. I had left a town with few opportunities outside of warehouse work and call centres, and, for all the displacement I felt at Cambridge, I had loved it as a place of fantasy. After university I felt affronted and naive when my friends joined graduate schemes in accounting, marketing and law, as though the ideal world I had entered was for some of them a stepping stone, a short intellectual holiday that led, ultimately, to reassimilation. The idea that no one would pay me to be good at analysing modernist literature came (surprisingly) as a shock. What had it all been for?

From home, my parents would call me each week in London, expecting the news that I had been offered a job, and each week I had to let them down. In the end, I moved home and took a job as a Christmas temp in a supermarket. It was tedious, utterly normal, everything I thought I had freed myself from. My only reprieve was in reading novels on the rickety bus on cold dark mornings, and again on the long journeys home. Gradually, I managed to save up enough money to go abroad. My thinking was that I couldn't be accused of being unsuccessful if I was travelling – at least I would be doing *something*. I wasn't done with my escaping yet.

I booked a trip to Colombia, much to the concern of my family, whose only associations with the country were through images on the news of balaclava'd drug gangs and homeland terrorism. Still, it was the cheapest long-haul flight I could find. I didn't have the money to be picky. During my breaks at work, in the staff canteen, I started to teach myself Spanish, and the following year I left the cold January of northern England and traded it for the blistering heat of Bogotá. When I arrived I felt lonelier than ever. My skin was deathly pale after months of English winter and I burnt within half an hour of being outside. I kept to the shaded side of the busy streets, avoiding the gaze of the passers-by, and began to wonder if doing nothing here was really better than doing nothing at home.

After a few days, conscious of being conspicuous as a loner in the hostel where I was staying, I decided to get a bus out of the city to a small town called Popayán. I had no idea where I was going, but I heard that, compared to Bogotá – which was disorientating, busy, and had a constant air of (real or imagined) threat – Popayán was quiet, eased by heat rather than agitated by it. When I boarded the night bus, the driver videoed my face, saying aloud the security number of the vehicle, then allowed me to climb up and find my seat. Everywhere I felt I was being watched. I only managed to get a few hours of sleep on the bus, and was woken around sunset by the light just burning up the edge of the hills and filling the valleys. There were palms, huge copses of bamboo, hills sectioned with fruit farms, and countless rundown villages made up of concrete houses and corrugated steel.

The route from the city of Cali to Popayán traversed a number of military checkpoints, so that every so often six or seven men came up from behind sandbags to give their thumbs up (or thumbs down) to the driver. But in Popayán things seemed more relaxed. The town was webbed with narrow streets that led down to the Plaza Mayor, which had a large square garden in the centre, stacked with tall palm trees. At night the street lamps glowed yellow, and the heat of the day lingered in the moist air, humming with insects. I spent a few days alone, wandering through the tiendas, picking through boxes of souvenirs and snacking on street food.

When the afternoon sun was too hot I went to one of the cafés off the main square, which had terraces dappled with leaf-shadow, or dipped into the cool emptiness of one of the churches. Sitting outside at noon I could almost feel the heat opening cracks in the whitewashed walls. Everywhere I went I carried a battered copy of *Tom Jones* with me, its Bible-thin paper fluttering when I tried to hold it open and eat my lunch at the same time. The book was old enough, strange enough, to make me feel as though I hadn't left everything behind. With it in hand, I felt that I was making use of myself, carrying a part of me from university out into the years, as if, through its pages, I could stem the tide of the world against myself. My individuality seemed so caught up with academia that I wasn't quite sure how to frame it once I'd graduated. Still, that bawdy, picaresque novel seemed to fit oddly well alongside the slow guitars and the rum-drinking of Popayán, the women who sat out in the mornings, resting their legs in the sun. I slipped in and out of it easily, caught in a foreigner's uncorrected fantasy, imagining myself in a time that slid neatly alongside Fielding's.

Really, I was eager to get moving: my plan was to go south from Popayán and then to journey further inland to the edge of the Amazon. I wasn't chasing anything but atmosphere, the imagined picturesque I wanted to exist in. I wanted the noise of forests, to feel broken light and endless falling water. On my last night in the town, I drank aguardiente in El Sotareño, then went back to the dormitory of the guest house, where my backpack was slung over the rail of my bunk bed. I moved it aside, cramming my creased clothes back in, and climbed into the lower bunk. I pulled the sheet over my head, trying to block out enough light to get to sleep. There were only a few other men staying in the dormitory, so it was generally quiet, but close to dawn I was woken by the noise of the door opening and someone stumbling into the room with heavy luggage. I looked up and saw him unpacking.

He had tanned skin and long, dark brown hair. I watched quietly as he arranged his things, climbed into the top bunk and fell to sleep. He was youthful in the way all tanned boys are. I saw him dreamily and watched him for a while, and then dozed back to sleep. When, a few weeks later, I first got close enough to smell him, he smelt of linen, like someone whose mother spoilt him. I think that made me feel safe, which is strange to say, but true. There was also his confidence, even his aloofness, his easy sociability.

Even that first time I saw him, I wanted to be near him, to fall under his warmth. When I woke an hour or so later, the sun was bright through the window. I could feel its heat on my face and my head was dulled with it. I clambered from the bed and walked over to the communal bathroom, where I washed under the cold tap, splashing the water over my face to cool it, then dressed, holding a towel around myself and watching in case the stranger's eyes opened and caught me in the middle of changing.

He looked so peaceful when he was sleeping, with the morning light inching its way along his body. Before I left, I walked over to the window and drew the blinds so that the sun, which was already hot and bright, wouldn't be on his face. That was one thing we always remembered afterwards. *He drew the blinds so I could sleep*, Elias would say, and I would nod, *I drew the blinds so he could sleep, he looked so peaceful*, as though I knew it was the beginning of something even then. Everyone loved this part of the story – the hot sun on terracotta roofs, all the white buildings gleaming in the squares, the dome of the basilica against the blue sky and the mountains. Even as we told it, it didn't seem like something that would happen to us, it felt like a novel.

I saw him later in the morning, eating breakfast at the plastic table in the courtyard, and smiled. There were tattoos along the nape of his neck that I hadn't noticed before when his long hair was down – together, they looked like a vine, with flowers blooming up into his hairline. I don't remember how I introduced myself, or whether it was anything so formal as that, but I learnt his name, that he was from Sweden, and that he was travelling alone. I had become much more at home in myself, but the question of how to approach another man – and more importantly how to gauge if he, like me, was interested – was one I deliberated over and over again. I stood by the table, nervously talking to him while he pulled apart some dry bread and dipped it into a sachet of honey. Between lines of conversation, I tried to catch a glance at him, to see if his friendliness was just gentleness or whether it was laced with something more urgent and questioning. Months later, Elias told me that, on

that first meeting at the breakfast table in the sunlit courtyard, he was nervous about me, too. Both of us were
escaping something. Both of us were wary about what we
were looking for.

Still, travelling was made up of brief friendships, crushes,
goodbyes, and I didn't expect to see him again. At 10 a.m. I
had to check out of the hostel. Carrying my rucksack, I
started the long walk through the hot town to the bus station, keeping to the shaded side of the quiet streets. At the
station, people clambered towards me, holding my arm,
trying to sell me tickets. *A dónde va? Amigo, amigo! Aqui,
aqui!* I didn't know where to look, and felt a horrible guilt
that I would have to choose only one, ashamed of this sudden awareness of power. I shook my head and looked down,
walking quickly over to the kiosks and asking, in bad Spanish, '*Cuanto cuesta à Mocoa?*' Eventually, I found a decent
price and a comfy chair I could fit in, and handed my bag
over to the driver.

On the small coach to the edge of the rainforest, I read
Tom Jones on the back seat, but I nearly hit my head on the
roof every time we went over a bump in the uneven road,
and after a while I gave up and closed my eyes. I drifted in
and out of sleep, thinking of Elias, his tattooed neck, his
tanned skin, his easy smile. I wondered how far that vine
travelled along his spine, and whether I'd see him again.
Then, on and on, the roads dwindling into smaller tracks,
the forest thickening at the windows. Occasionally, there
were roadside cafés, petrol stations, clearings in the woods
full of cattle. I bought a skewer of meat from a boy grilling
them under the corrugated roof of a concrete house. After I
had finished, I asked him if it was beef. He shook his head,
pointed at my chest and said, '*Corazón!*'

I got back on the coach, feeling queasy, and tried my best to sleep. Between one dream and the next, an old woman boarded the coach with a plastic bag of *maracujas*, and handed one to each passenger with a smile, before taking her seat. I thanked her and took one, grateful for the kindness, the extension of camaraderie. We stopped, eventually, just outside Mocoa, a small jungle town in Putamayo. I had rented a little cabin on a site full of trees and, after picking up the keys, I bought some beers and sat out on the concrete lip of the veranda, listening to the pulsing beat of the insects humming through the rainforest. Just beyond the perimeter of the site there were creeks and waterfalls separated by warm, deep, swimming holes; trees dripping in rain showers and hot, humid mist. Everything was constantly dappled with sun, shards of brightness reflecting off the water and the slick leaves. It was so alive, so awake. My first night there I had a vivid dream of a circus. There were acrobats and clowns and fire-throwers spinning at the window, a raucous band of them, and when I woke the clashing and burring and shrieking went on outside in the darkness of the forest.

In the morning my head buzzed with the heat and the noise, but when I opened the window it made no difference: the air was still, heavy, immovable. I drank some water from a half-empty gallon bottle and opened the door to put on my boots, which I'd left overnight to dry on the step outside. I sat down on the step and moved to pick up the first boot, but as I touched it, a loud, percussive noise drummed out of it and I started back. I tried to kick the boot over, quickly, then step back, but nothing appeared. Then the sound stopped. A silence amongst the humming of the forest, like a newly opened emptiness in my perception. Just a boot lying sole-side-up on the concrete veranda. Maybe, I thought, the noise wasn't coming from inside the shoe at all. I looked around. The wood was singing itself awake under the sun – everything calling, a riot of sound. And here was my boot – lifeless, empty, tipped up, and me prickling with a sort of stupid, nervous anticipation. When finally I plucked up the courage to take hold of the boot and shake it, out dropped a tiny beetle, no more than an inch long, which ruffled itself on the concrete and then scuttled off over the ridge and into the wet grass.

Someone had hung a branch of bananas over a nail on the corner-post of the lodge, gradually ripening from the bottom upwards like a chromatic scale. I took two from the bottom of the clutch and walked off in my sandals down to where the stream was gushing into the pools between the rocks. Clambering down on to the smooth stones, which were already hot with the sun, I slipped my feet into the water. They were still starkly white, and where the pool rippled they were taken out of perspective into a weird, enlarged world. The water was cool, so I took off my top and slid in. It was so deep I struggled to touch the bottom and bobbed awkwardly, floating like a bowling pin, ducking my head and then shaking off my hair, looking around at the forest and the few people already gathering upstream with their towels and breakfasts.

Even in these quiet moments I was afraid of purposelessness. After a half hour or so just floating in the pool, I pulled myself up on to the warm rock and stretched out, the water drying off me almost instantly. I read *Tom Jones* for a while – there was some trouble happening and Tom had broken his arm – but after only half a chapter I got up, distracted by the noise of the water and the birds, and decided to follow the streams into the forest, up a hill path to where the water was crashing down from. All the trees were dripping wet, full of squawks and wild laughing, and by the time I reached the top my clothes were soaked through, whether with sweat or with the humidity, it was hard to tell.

When I reached the top of the hill there was a sheer drop into a deep pool, with the water shivering white at the edge, splashing up and breaking into jewels, then falling in an almighty, constant crash as it spilled over the fall. 'Fin del Mundo' or 'The End of the World' was what the locals called it. I'd seen photos of it back in the hostel in Popayán. You could lie down before you reached the drop, and shimmy forwards with your hands and elbows, dragging yourself to the brink, so that only your head poked out over the top, and you were horizontal, aligned with the heavy-falling river, watching it hurtling down. I put the book away and stripped to my swimming shorts, then stepped carefully into the water, keeping low to the riverbed, scared of falling and being carried off by the current. I lay down and pulled myself slowly towards the horizontal line where the water rushed and fell, until I was looking over the edge. My stomach clenched at the sight of the drop, the rocks being battered endlessly by the river, and I could almost feel my own body down there on the stones, being battered, too.

Then I heard a few voices behind me – a group of boys walking up the path to the edge. I turned around and, to my surprise, recognised one of them. It was Elias, wearing a black tank top, the cotton stuck to his glistening shoulders. I didn't know whether he'd remember me or not, though it had only been a few days, and so I kept my head down for a while, watching the water, suddenly self-conscious, aware of my body, thinking of how I might get back from the edge of the waterfall without having to awkwardly drag myself in reverse over the shallow riverbed. Eventually, he must have noticed me and called out my name, so then I had to pretend not to have noticed him at all, feigning shock and a smile, pulling myself up and walking over to him, the front of my T-shirt damp and covered with soil and green stains. If he recognised me, then he remembered me. That must mean something, I thought.

We shook hands – it seems oddly formal, now, remembering that first shaking of hands – and I told him to go over to the edge of the waterfall just the way I'd done it. I stood, watching him awkwardly dragging himself forward, and then heard his gasp and his deep, excited laugh echoing over the cliff-edge as he peered down. He wasn't afraid, even among strangers, of how loud his own laugh was. He was easy in his own enjoyment, not embarrassed of it. The other boys – three Australians and a Dane – followed suit, and soon there was a row of them, all face-down on the forest floor, looking over the edge of the waterfall, giggling at their own fear, teasing and pretending to push each other or shouting 'Boo!' and then breaking into a riot of laughter if any of the others jumped in fright. I never knew how to act around straight men, but I loved that giddy, boyish delight. It gave me a sense of something less restrained, less self-conscious, under the surface of their masculinity.

After the excitement had subdued, they shimmied back from the edge and we all sat around the shallow green pools at the top of the fall – some of the boys kicking their feet in the water, others chattering away, pulling leaves from the trees around them, and watching them float off into the water, then shudder suddenly with the taut current, before being drawn over the edge. I tried to catch a look at

Elias – the flowers on his neck, which looked like roses; his long biceps, his smooth, tanned legs. Occasionally, I thought I could feel him looking at me, glancing at me; other times it was just the strange almost-sensation of the light from the river refracting its rays across my skin. I watched as Elias lay down on his back in one of the stiller pools for a while, taking deep breaths and then lowering his head, so the pool seemed to swallow him and then close over his face. I wanted to know him.

Later that evening, after a few drinks, he told me how he could hear the voices of the boys underwater, distorted, and the sounds of the moisture dripping from the palm fronds on to the surface, as though everything were going on around him. He heard the voices inside the water, and the bubbling crashes of the stream and the grinding of the stones, and, lost in the echoes, briefly forgot himself. It was like being in a different world, he said, like being submerged in another dimension.

*

A few weeks later, Elias and I found ourselves drunk at a beach bar in Peru, the sound of reggaeton bouncing over the dance floor. We'd been in the same town together for a week, but staying in different hostels, and he had been elusive, non-committal. He would turn up at parties and in bars and talk to me, introducing me to his friends, but then I'd lose him again. I got the impression that he knew I liked him and that he was trying to put some distance between himself and me. I knew the pattern: a kind straight boy recognises my attention, wants to be cool and gentle with my desire, and then begins to avoid me, afraid of getting too close. I'd resigned myself to it many times over, though each time it happened I failed to realise what was going on until it was too late and I would embarrass myself. Elias seemed to fit the pattern, so I tried to meet him with a mirror of his own aloofness, to be cool, to act as though I hadn't spent every intervening hour anticipating the next time I'd see him.

We sat outside the bar talking for a while, drinking rum, and a trader came over with a box of cigarettes and cigars, offering them to us. I took a long cigarillo, intrigued, and the man lit it for me and I thanked him. Elias was trying to teach me Swedish, and would occasionally point to things and give me the word for them: beer was *öl*; a chair was *en stol*. When the man came over, I learnt that a cigarette was basically the same, *en cigarett*. I said each word back to Elias, waiting for him to approve my attempt at pronunciation.

'*En cigarrrrett*', he said, holding out his hand to emphasise the trilling of his tongue. When I said it again, he shook his head and smiled. 'English people can't roll their *r*'s'.

'That's not true,' I said, my fragile pride affronted. I trilled my tongue against my palate. 'See! Rrrrrrrrr.' I thought I'd proved my point, but he laughed again, his eyes holding mine for a while.

'You're thinking of Americans,' I said. 'English people can roll their *r*'s. Give me a word,' I said, 'and I'll show you.'

Elias was wearing a linen shirt, his face glowing from the day's sun, and his hair was pushed back behind his ears. He was easy and didn't seem at all daunted by my familiarity, so I began to think that his previous aloofness was just a projection of my own insecurity.

There were no bathrooms inside the bar, and as the night wore on we had watched people begin to stumble more frequently down the sandy road towards the beach, where it was dark enough to go to the toilet without being seen. Elias looked around for a second, and at first I thought he was checking out the other people, but then I realised he was looking for something, trying to find another noun to give me. A waiter walked past, carrying plates. Elias looked back at me, mischievously, and said '*Räkor.*'

'What's that?'

'Prawns.'

I laughed. 'OK.' I gave it my best go, rolling both *r*'s on my tongue, trying not to get distracted by them.

'*Vad duktig du är!*' he said, slapping my arm firmly and smiling.

I was uncomfortable at being patronised, and felt that the new phrase was a way of proving how little I knew. I rolled my eyes. 'What does that mean?'

He stuttered for a second, thinking to himself, but came up short. 'I don't think you have a word for *duktig* in English,' he said. 'It means *to be good at something, to be a quick learner.*'

I wracked my brain to think of a word we might have, as though to prove my prowess. *Adept, accomplished, clever* . . . None of them seemed to fit the bill. In the end, I conceded.

'*Duktig,*' I said, and he nodded, and I found I was happy to have regained his approval.

I was enjoying being alone with him, having him to myself, and he seemed to like teaching me, so I looked around for ways to extend the game. There was something new and intimate in having him give me words, in feeling the strange ways they made my mouth work, as though he were imparting something to me, as though we were beginning to build an understanding between us, a secret code that could be ours. He thought of some more words and phrases that foreigners found difficult to say, words with difficult sounds. The '*y*' and the '*sj*' of Swedish, he said, were markers of a non-native speaker. I found that he was so good at English that I didn't think I had anything to offer him in return.

After a while, the game lost its joy through repetition, and Elias had finished his drink and begun to look around, impatiently now. His eyes were darting occasionally over my shoulder, so I turned, but didn't recognise any of the people there.

'Are you looking for someone?'

He shook his head.

'I need to go to the beach', he said. That phrase, in the small town we were in, was already a euphemism for needing the bathroom. 'Want to come?'

On the beach the sound of the music from the street quickly emptied into the gentle crashing of the sea. From the dark mid-distance, people stumbled back towards the lights of the bars, struggling through the loose, dry sand. It was hard to tell how far we'd have to walk before we couldn't be seen, but both of us were drunk, and, as we went further towards the sea, Elias seemed to forget about needing the bathroom at all. My flip-flops kept sliding under my feet and were throwing sand up behind me with every step. Elias's were doing the same. I took mine off and held them in my hands while I walked, the sand cool beneath my feet and the ocean turning over in its bed, still too far off to be seen.

After a while, Elias sat down on the sand, then lay back with his hands under his head, looking at the open sky. I sat down next to him and looked up at the sky, too. Elias breathed in deeply, as though he was on the brink of some deep philosophical question and didn't know how to formulate it aloud. I turned to him, anticipating it. He didn't look at me, but let out a faintly audible sigh. Then he opened his mouth and took a moment before he spoke, his eyes still raised to the sky.

'Do you know what the Danish people call flip-flops?' he said, deadpan.

I looked at him and laughed. 'That wasn't what I was expecting you to say.' I wasn't sure if he was setting up a joke or whether he'd wanted to tell me something else, but chickened out at the last minute. 'No, Elias,' I said, 'I don't know what Danish people call flip-flops.' By this point I was becoming impatient, tired of having my desire teased and then let down.

'Do you want to know?'

I sighed and looked at him. 'Yes. I suppose I do now.'

He paused for emphasis before he answered. '*Klippklapper.*'

He laughed to himself as he said it again, shaking his head. '*Klippklapper!*'

I didn't know if it was a Scandinavian in-joke or just the truth, but soon I was laughing at him laughing, and I was in love then with his unpredictable joy. I leant briefly against his shoulder and he turned to me and looked for a long moment into my eyes, and then the laughter stopped and suddenly we were kissing and I couldn't believe it was happening. Everything I thought I had invented, every glance of his, every casual touch, was confirmed in an instant.

The next morning I woke up in my bed with the mosquito net knotted above me and Elias next to me, fast asleep.

I had a rash of insect bites along my bare leg. His skin was hot against mine and his shirt was stuck to his back, damp with sweat. I felt as though I had pulled some figment of a dream back into real life with me: the night before had happened and he was there, lying next to me, like the proof of some unlikely and secret miracle. Then, after I went to shower, I came back and found he was gone.

Over the next few days I would see him occasionally, sitting outside bars with his friends or walking back from his morning swim, but he was never alone. People seemed to cluster around him, to look at him adoringly as he spoke. One girl, who was also Swedish, and whom I had been not-so-subtly grilling for information about him, told me that Elias was nothing like the other Swedes. They were quiet, shy, reticent about new people, but he was full of stories and seemed to put everyone at ease. He was usually the loudest person in any group. Quickly, though, I saw that it wasn't from arrogance, but from a sense of duty in keeping every conversation afloat with laughter. He seemed so worldly to me, so confident, and it was good to be around him. I was reserved sometimes and found new people difficult, but he made friends of everyone, so that soon there was a whole gang around him wherever he went.

Eventually, he started speaking to me again, inviting me to places, and there was a privilege, I thought, in being by his side, in feeling the glow of his charm reflected on to me. As, one by one, the other friends left to carry on their travels or to go home, the group dwindled over a fortnight until it was just Elias and me left, and he became more direct, more open to the idea of me. We were never a secret from the others, but both of us instinctively felt the need to hide ourselves in public. There was something exciting about it:

kissing after the lights went out in the dorms, or sneaking into the shower cubicles together when the hostels were empty. He made it feel like an adventure, as if we were two co-conspirators and what we had was only our own.

I had booked a return flight from Bogotá, and was supposed to be travelling in a circle, following the coast back up to Colombia, but when I learnt that Elias was travelling south, I changed my route and pretended I had always been planning to go in the same direction. So we took a bus across the border to Bolivia together, and the weeks drifted into months and, before I knew it, I was completely in love. It all happened so quickly, magnified by the fact that we travelled alone together, ate every meal together, and slept together every night. The sort of intimacy that would have taken a year to gain in our normal lives seemed to be established in a matter of weeks, and when finally I had to leave him, two months later, and take a series of night buses back through Peru, Ecuador and then Colombia, I felt as though I had left a newly discovered part of myself behind.

*

Back at home, in the early days of summer, I got a part-time job as a waiter, and would anxiously check my phone between shifts. Elias would send photos from South America. I missed him to the point of distraction: I couldn't focus on work, and the weeks seemed to pass slowly towards the date we'd arranged, after he got back to Sweden, when I would go to visit him. Somehow, we both thought we could keep the relationship going, but I didn't know how. I hadn't got enough money to travel often, and I had to move to Liverpool that September to start a new degree. Regardless, I felt like what we had was too precious to let practicalities get in the way. The whole thing was built on hopes and idealism. Real life was something that people lived when they weren't in love, and I wouldn't pay it much heed if I could help it.

I was afraid that, once I saw Elias again in Gothenburg, his home town, things would be different. Perhaps being home would bring him back to his senses. South America had been a fantasy world where things could happen, and the cold shock of coming back to work, to friends, to family, would make him realise how impractical being together would be. When the date came, I went to the airport with a nagging sense of my own naivety. How innocent must I look to everyone around me, dragging my suitcase off to Sweden, following after a man I had only known for a few months?

When I boarded, the budget flight was crowded. I sat next to a mother and her son, my legs pushed to one side. The small plastic table I dropped down from the seat in front wouldn't sit flat across my knees, so I held my coffee and my book precariously as the flight shook its way across England and then over across the northern tip of Denmark. The pilot made announcements about the clear weather in Sweden, and eventually the air stewards took their seats. Outside, the wing of the plane tilted towards the sea, and I saw the edge of the land coming into view beneath a thin layer of cloud. There were hardly any lights down there, just trees. Unlike the endless fields of England, or the brown heather of the hills over high ground, which were the last things I saw as the plane took off from Manchester, below me now the land was barely visible – just the deep green of pines, and blue-black lakes glinting between them. The whole place looked uninhabited, and I wondered if Elias was down there, driving somewhere between the trees to the airport, the slip of the road invisible through the thick canopy.

After we landed, I collected my bag from the carousel, but was uneasy about stepping through the dividing doors into the arrivals lounge. I wasn't sure how to translate my feelings for Elias in such a public place. It was months since I'd seen him, and the airport was busy; people everywhere bustling through with suitcases, prams, rogue children running around, trying to sit on the luggage trolleys. After a few minutes standing there, trying to work up a sort of airy confidence, I merged with a crowd, taking cover amongst them, hoping I would see Elias before he saw me.

In the bustle of bodies, the faces waiting in the lounge came in flashes, but I couldn't see him anywhere. I pulled my suitcase behind me, away from the flow of the people, and stood by a kiosk where I could get a better view of the lounge. Then, just as I was pulling out my phone to text him, I heard his big, bright voice ringing out like a bell, and turned to see him bounding over to me, his hands held apart, a grin on his face.

'Hello, stranger!' he laughed, pulling me into him, and I laughed, too, partly out of shock at how loud he was, but mostly out of relief and the warmth on his face. It wasn't just in a foreign country that he was boisterous, then; even on home turf, in a hall of hundreds of people, he wasn't embarrassed of happiness or of me. When I went to hug him, I could smell that fresh linen smell I still remembered, the easy strength of his arms, the clean, soft press of his hair against my cheek.

'Come on,' he said, taking my luggage and throwing his arm around my back, guiding me towards the door. He looked somehow different, and I realised then that I'd only seen him in the same three or four outfits he'd taken travelling with him. 'You made it here all on your own,' he said. '*Vad duktig du är.*' He loved teasing me. He had sensed immediately my pride and how easily it was punctured, and I loved that I felt safe in letting him do it.

It was late as we walked out into the car park, but there was still a lingering warmth in the air. We would be staying at his parents' house, where he was still living, and Elias had borrowed his father's car to pick me up. The radio came on automatically as Elias started the engine, and he reached out and turned the volume down, as if to say that this time was for us, no interruptions, no other voices. As we pulled out of the airport, the landscape around us was an endless stretch of flat fields, and on the horizon thin woodlands made a dark laced silhouette against a yellow strip of light from a sun which still hadn't set. It was quiet in the car, and I talked nervously to fill the silence, telling him about the plane journey, how cramped it was, how busy it had been in Manchester, the rain at home, and, after a few minutes, he just turned his head to me and smiled.

'You're cute,' he said.

'Fuck off,' I said, blushing. I went quiet again, stilled by his confidence, in awe of how he could take the silence.

My eyes lingered, as he sped up along the straight empty road, on the veins on his forearm, the strength of his hand on the wheel. He felt so opposite to me, in a way that gave me a frisson of fear, but also a sense of wholeness. I had already dreamt up the idea that he could complement and adjust everything I lacked. Perhaps sensing that I was nervous, he reached his hand across to me, his eyes still on the road ahead, and I felt as though my body might give off a spark when he touched it. His hand was on my leg, and I reached out, too, and grasped his thigh, and felt the muscle tensing as he pressed on the accelerator. I think I was amazed and afraid that he was real, that there was something so easy as touching him, that I was allowed to, that he wanted to touch me too.

We were heading down a road that bent in the far distance into the pine woods and vanished. There were no other cars, no houses, no street lamps. Before we got to the forest, I felt the car slow down. Elias said nothing, until I realised he was pulling in to a layby at the side of the road.

'Why are we stopping here?' I asked, not catching on.

He turned to me mischievously and pulled the latch at the back of my chair, so it reclined beneath me. Then, smoothly, he undid his seatbelt and leant over to me, and suddenly all the tension and nerves sparked into an eager and deep kissing, a fumbling of belts, the rush of being back together.

By the time we were driving off again into the straight dark road, speeding off into the woods, I was exhausted and at peace – nothing but the summer air, no radio, just the quiet thump of the road and the fields behind us with a twinge of yellow-orange on the horizon, and the blue haze and the cloudless indigo sky.

*

We spent that month together, and Elias introduced me to more friends than I could keep count of. Everywhere we went in Gothenburg he knew someone, and it was wild to think that he had chosen me, that he was proud of me being there. At the end of August he said he would come back to England with me and get a job in Liverpool for a year, while I did my degree. My friends seemed to think I was being rash, moving too quickly, but I didn't care. It felt right and easy. I'd wanted for so long to have someone like him, and he never seemed to pause to question what we were doing, just went along with it, taking it all in his stride, so I knew that it must feel right for him, too.

When we moved to Liverpool it all felt so close to a real life – jobs and friends and our own place to live. In the mornings Elias would go out to work, and I would brew some coffee and sit at my desk with my writing and listen to the seagulls and the city beginning to rouse. Between books of poems and scrawled notepads, I was occasionally distracted by the people walking down the alleyway below the window, and after a while I realised there were more people going into the entrance opposite than seemed right. It was a black, windowless metal door, with no signage above it, just a security camera. Every day I would see people arrive, some in dresses, some in tracksuits, some in business attire. At first, I couldn't figure out what they were all doing, until one day I looked up the address online and found that it was advertised as a gay sauna. It became a running joke that I had picked the location of the apartment on purpose.

I was amazed by the city, that we might accidentally live so close to a place I would have never thought existed. I spent most days writing at my desk overlooking the alleyway, and over time some of the people began to wave up to me in the window on their way to and from the sauna, and I would wave back and smile at them. An unlikely sort of kinship, between the quiet student and the drag queens and the twinks, but it was my first real sense of community.

Sometimes, when Elias and I got home from a night out, I would go and sit with them on the steps in the alleyway and hear their gossip, and ask them what it was like inside the sauna, though I never plucked up the courage to go inside.

One morning I left our flat into the blustery, bright sunshine of a spring morning. A few drag queens were still out from the night before, heaped on the steps outside the sauna, cackling with each other. I waved to them as I locked the door behind me, laughing along with their catcalls as I pretended to mince along the cobblestones. I had a rucksack full of books to return to the library, and was jealous of their abandon. It was a glorious day and I decided to take a long detour, hailing the bus up to a university park where a friend had told me one of Hopkins's poems was carved into a stone. It didn't feel like a day for work: if the drag queens at the sauna were having a day off, why couldn't I?

When I got to the garden, I walked for a while trying to find it. There were small stones with lines of the poem ('Pied Beauty') on them, but my friend had told me that there was a block somewhere with the whole text. A heavy, warm shower of rain began to fall, and when finally I found the carved slab I stood over it and I watched as the grey stone was spotted with water. The rain filled up the grooves of the lettering, and the words seemed to be wakened by the touch of the water. The words 'Glory be to God for dappled things' were stippled all over with heavy drops, and the grey stone turned a shining darker shade as the shower covered it. Then, as quickly as it had started, the shower was over. Glory be to God, I thought, for rain, for the spring, for the sequined drag queens in the alleyway. For 'fresh-firecoal chestnut-falls; finches' wings', for Hopkins, for

Elias and I and our new life, for all things 'counter, original, spare, strange'.

*

At the end of my degree, a year later, I got a scholarship to study for a doctorate, and Elias wanted to go back to university, too. He had dropped out of an architecture course some years earlier and thought he might give it another shot. So, we agreed that we would move to Gothenburg, for the summer and autumn at least, and I would try working remotely, writing and researching my thesis and flying back to Liverpool every month to go to the library and pick up books.

That summer in Gothenburg, before I started my PhD, I got used to the long nights when the sun barely dipped the horizon before lifting again into the sky. It was hot, dry weather for months. We lived in the downstairs of his parents' house in the suburbs, where there was a bedroom and a small kitchenette, so we could come and go without disturbing them. Elias asked around and got me a job, so in the evenings I worked on the terrace of an expensive restaurant, where I wore a white suit with blue lapels and gold epaulettes that made me look like a cruise ship entertainer. The nights were late and, if we got to sleep at all, we were woken by the sun at 3 a.m. Even the birds barely rested their singing from one day to the next.

I was learning Swedish, mostly, through living it – waiting tables in the restaurant, talking to Elias's family, overhearing conversations at parties and on the radio. I had a store of phrases and answers, things I could cling to. Over time I had got the grasp of grammar and my mistakes became less frequent, and the sentences had begun to form themselves more fluidly, coming not from conscious thought, but somehow emerging from my mouth almost intact. Still, there were times when I came unstuck. How did something make me feel? I could say it made me happy or sad or excited, but when it came to explaining why, or explaining any emotion that fell between – or combined – those blunt categories, I was left stuttering, embarrassed, frustrated. I'd lift my arms, shake my head, exhale, and then say it in English, which was always an easy get-out. The sentences I could make from Swedish wouldn't bend the way I needed them to. I didn't have the grammar for abstract things.

Most Swedes spoke English with a fluency that seemed totally natural. That in itself made learning Swedish hard. When I didn't know the meaning of the name of an item on the menu in the restaurant, the customers always offered it up without much thought. It was so easy for me to give up, to revert back to my mother tongue. That summer with Elias, I sometimes worried that we were simplifying ourselves for each other. I became strangely conscious that I could only say the things I had the language for. It felt as though I were learning again, as I had as a child, to make myself verbal.

Outside of work, we'd spend the days getting the bus out to the lakes or to the archipelago. Elias's friends had no problem swimming naked, and I got used to it after a while – the pile of clothes left on the rocks, the quick run and the soaring moment before the body crashed down into the black water and shattered it. Those days, the lakes were like glass hammered by the sun – flat, glinting magnificently, and underneath the brown, cool depths full of silt and lovely, soft mud. Elias, full of bravado, would strip off quickly, not pausing to check if people could see him. Then, he'd dive straight in, yelping sometimes from the cold.

'Come on!' he'd shout.

I was shy and unused to being naked around other people, but how could I not follow him? He'd dive down into the brown water, the pale skin of his legs vanishing for a while, then bob back up again and shake his hair, and I wanted so much to be in there with him, to have his boyish ebullience.

I loved swimming over to him and wrapping my legs around him, playfighting in the water, then pulling up on to the rocks. Sometimes we'd walk off into the woods, the bright pine needles and the soft green moss under our feet, and Elias would show me which mushrooms you could eat. He seemed so at home there, so full of a knowledge not taken from books, but from life. Once, we came out when the woods were full of yellow chanterelles. '*Skogens guld*,' he said. 'The forest's gold.'

Because July and August were spent in what I remember as an endless sunshine, when October arrived the change in the weather felt sudden and pronounced. In Sweden it was as though the year existed in two seasons only. Instead of winter turning gradually to spring, through summer and autumn and back again, this year we were given night and day – one all darkness, the other all light. As we passed into autumn, all down the long avenues of the city the trees began to curl, the tips of the leaves singed with the cold. All of a sudden, my mornings in the city were spent in dark, candle-lit cafés. I would wake next to Elias, still sleeping beside me, then walk out on to the streets in my long coat, scarf wrapped high under my chin, through the woods on the hill and down to the library, or to a small café off Götaplatsen that sold strong filter coffee and played Billie Holiday on a seemingly endless loop. In the encroachment of autumnal mist and the pewter light, even ordering a coffee at such a quiet hour felt vaguely conspiratorial. I was writing a chapter about Hopkins, his sermons and his diaries, and for the first few hours of each morning, I'd sit with my notes spread out on the table, and type a page or two, taking my time over a few lines, an unusual rhyme in a sonnet, some piece of idiosyncratic theology I had yet to pin down.

The problem I always felt with reading Hopkins was that, in the best way possible, reading his poems made me not want to be reading them. They were full of a bouncing, riotous energy. Something in the rhythms, the clashes and uncertainties of the syntax, thrilled a voltage through my body, and I wanted to throw the book down and run outside to look at something, to see the world as he made me see it. He had started his training as a Jesuit in Manresa House in Birmingham, where the men were given 'modesty powder' to make their bathwater opaque, and had surprised his fellow trainees by his sharp mind, his effeminacy and his strangeness. When he was supposed to be cleaning outdoor latrines, he was distracted by the frost patterns that his fellow men's urine had made on the stones. The poem I was reading, a sonnet called 'The Starlight Night', was written in the same year that he was ordained, and was so ecstatic that it was hard to sit still while I read it. It was as though Hopkins were there, shouting at me for being inside, for doing anything so dull as reading a book.

Look at the stars! look, look up at the skies!
    O look at all the fire-folk sitting in the air!
    The bright boroughs, the circle-citadels there!
Down in dim woods the diamond delves! the elves'-eyes!

I could almost feel him dragging me by the scruff of my neck outside. It seemed so contradictory to be sitting there in a dark café, puzzling out some piece of theology or metre, when the poem itself was telling me to get up, to go out and look at how beautiful the world was.

Still, that autumn, the city seemed to lend itself to a sense of the occluded and the hermetic. The world had started to whisper. The people began to stay inside, away from the cold of the streets, and sometimes the fog was so dense it would press up against the window, and there were mornings I'd wake to the light eerie and orange against the glass. The air steeled, turned grey or blue-grey, sharpened with frost. The city felt like an entirely different place to the one we'd spent the summer in. When I'd come home for lunch, or meet Elias in town if he'd been to class, we'd eat something cheap – fried pyttipanna with mayonnaise, or some pre-packed skagenröra on rye bread – then sit in in our room as the day outside sank into night not long past three o'clock.

I would carry on with my reading on the sofa, and Elias would go back to bed or watch TV on his laptop, wearing his headphones so I could carry on with work. Occasionally, I would glance over at him, full of longing. He seemed so peaceful in his quietness, his long taut body, his tangle of hair tied up; but I was so unused to him not talking, not enthusing about something, that I began again to wonder if he wanted me like I wanted him. He seemed to have cooled off, become more introspective, and I couldn't figure out what I'd done wrong. Eventually, when he didn't look over, I would go back to my work, back to Hopkins, to a far-off, cloistered world of oratories, churches, mountains, and forget, briefly, that things seemed to have changed between us.

With the darkness and the weather and his schedule of

lectures and workshops, it hardly seemed strange that Elias slept for longer, or that he was sometimes harder to rouse. The city itself had fallen into something like a blackout, as though everyone were in hiding. Everything slept for longer. Even the sun was reluctant, and showed its face only late in the day, if at all. I hardly noticed it at first, but it dawned on me that for weeks Elias had been asking me, implicitly, what life was for. A strange, philosophical tack had come into his conversation. The day to day had been replaced by the abstract, the conjectural. I should have noticed them, all the usual signs – not wanting to see his friends, self-doubt, worrying away about work, about the future. I thought it was my fault, that a future with me was becoming harder and harder to imagine. At least, he seemed not to be able to do it any more, as though he couldn't seem to fit himself into the picture. I wondered where the easy Elias of that summer had gone, and if I'd done something to push him away.

So, without being conscious of it at first, I had been trying for weeks to convince him that life – just *life*, in all its vague abstractness – was worth it, just because.

'You don't have to do anything you don't want to do,' I said one morning, trying to get him out of bed. 'Just be with your friends, or on your own. Don't worry about me. Eat what you like, go where you like. Just come on, put on some clothes, have some coffee, come for a walk. Just down the road to the woods, only a little walk. We won't see anyone. It'll be fine, just the two of us, like we used to do, just little things.' I would say, 'Don't worry about anything. I'm here with you, all the way.' But no matter what I said, it didn't work. The problem was both bigger and more diffuse than I could imagine.

I was scared by how things had altered, and by the things Elias had begun to think, which were so unlike him. Eventually, even the small worries became extreme and I couldn't get a foothold in their logic.

'Everyone I love will leave me,' he said, over and over again.

'What do you mean? I won't leave you. Elias, look at me. Look. I'm not going anywhere.'

After a few days of this, I felt my eyes blur with tears whenever he started again. I was so confused at not being able to pinpoint what had happened.

'Hush, hush, don't be silly,' I'd say, 'of course not.' Or I would say, 'Don't think about the big questions now, they're not important. Just take it day by day, hour by hour. Everything will be just fine, trust me,' holding his hand and whispering into his ear, holding his face to my chest, his long hair between my fingers, and feeling the warmth of his breath like a child, and eventually, terrifyingly, his tears against my shirt.

As best as I could, I tried to shine the world for him, as though I could convince him out of whatever strange logic had taken hold. I would spend hours putting my case together, collecting evidence in my mind. Lists of things that were wonderful: evenings in the park with friends; snow on a bright day; swimming in the lake in summertime; even just sitting here together. Wasn't that something? It was more than I had ever thought was possible. Sometimes, in the process, the more I talked, the more I'd end up making it all less and less convincing, even for myself. Words seemed to unravel the spell of life. I'd lie awake at night with his voice in my head, asking myself, *Is that it? Is that everything?*

But then, a new day came and a new distraction, and I'd flit back to work or to whatever else was to be done, and the voice in my head would go quiet, and I'd forget that perhaps the voice in his head was persistent, ongoing, still nagging in its sharp, undermining way. Life went on, I thought – Elias waking to go to lectures, returning home for lunch, his drawings under his arm, and sometimes little balsa wood models of houses – but after a while, he started to get into bed when the night came in the late afternoon, and I was left to my daily task of trying to navigate my new life in a foreign country, suddenly alone.

Gothenburg, for all its industrial past, was picturesque. There were cobbled streets in the old town of Haga, each of which was lined with wooden houses and bakeries. The town was laid out with urban canals I would walk along to meet Elias after his lectures, and some days, as he slept, I went out alone to Slottsskogen, a large park on the town's outer limit, where moose and fallow deer still roamed through the pines and the birches. Even in the suburbs close to the city, where we lived, it was not unusual to be standing by the kitchen window and see a roe deer hop through the shrubbery, or to see hares wandering along the pavements into the woods that scattered the hillsides. There was a magic in it all that was more than enough to keep me invested in life, and I was frustrated that Elias couldn't see it.

The people, I found, were nothing like the Elias I had known before I came here. They were quiet, almost furtive, unused to speaking to strangers. What our friends in South America had said seemed to be right: Elias was nothing like a Swede. He was confident and chatty and open. In winter, the Swedes kept indoors, tucked away, and life in

Gothenburg became cold and isolating. Each day, around three or four o'clock, night began seeping down to the horizon, where the pines seemed almost to smoke their shadows over the houses. Every day Elias was turning in earlier and earlier, tired (I told myself) from work, and I remember walking out of the house each night after dinner, taking the track over the hillsides and through the woods, with the lamplight glowing orange through the fog and each branch hung with jewels of half-frozen dew. The air was cold and beaded, and the place seemed completely empty, only me walking in my heavy coat and the shattered water lilting between the trees. And then I'd turn home, unlock the door, and Elias would be sitting awake, the blue light of the laptop screen making something ghostly of his tired, hollowing face.

It might seem strange that I didn't register the change in the way I should have, but the blurring from past happiness into present dissatisfaction – or worse – was incremental, stepping along in tiny gradations, shading slowly from white through grey and on into black. I say that everything seemed gradual, or that it seemed to suit the tenor of the encroaching season, not to excuse myself from having let things go unnoticed, but because I can only see the tipping point in hindsight. The accrual of symptoms, the increasing desperation that Elias felt, did not change day to day, but week to week, month to month. It had been happening long before I realised. Like in a game of grandmother's footsteps, it was as though I had stood facing a wall, fixated on it, and all the while a new life had crept up silently behind me.

One day blurred into another, and normality reset its gauge in secret, without my noticing. At some point, Elias went to the doctor and was prescribed some medication. I took hope in his being proactive, though I admit now that there was a deeper part of me that thought this was all a bit dramatic. I told one friend over the phone about the prescription, and she scoffed: 'Doctors prescribe pills for anything these days.' Part of me thought the same. He didn't seem that bad, surely. Perhaps I agreed, or perhaps I didn't want to admit that my perfect dream was collapsing around me, that I wasn't enough to help him by myself.

So, on the morning of his twenty-seventh birthday, at his parents' house in the suburbs, I sat with him on the sofa, drinking coffee, and watched him cry. I didn't know what to do any more, because I still didn't know what was wrong. I was looking for a reason and couldn't find one. It was like trying to shoot a cloud with an arrow. There was desperation in his eyes. As he looked at me, it was as though he were looking into me from another world, trying to reach across some void, but everything he said was somehow falling short, not quite carrying its meaning across. He told me he felt worse, much worse, not just gradually worse but perceptibly, definitely worse.

'Worse than last week?' I asked.

'Yes.'

'Worse than yesterday?'

'I think so.'

After some insistence on my part, he agreed that he should call the doctor, to ask about the tablets and how they should be working. Was it normal that after a fortnight of taking them he should feel not better, but infinitely more hopeless than when he started? Surely that couldn't be right.

The receptionist told him that the doctor was in a meeting and would call back soon. It was when we were making breakfast, and Elias was packing his bag for university, that the phone rang. He grabbed his rucksack and his mobile and went downstairs. I heard him pick up the phone, say hello, and then begin chatting. The conversation drifted out of earshot, so I went back to watching the eggs boiling and turning in the pot, standing in the shafts of autumn sunlight breaking through the branches of the garden's one crooked apple tree, and thinking of his birthday lunch later that afternoon, what we would order, and what I would do with myself in the meantime.

*

His father had driven us into the city, and we had stood in the car park of the university for a while, Elias promising that he wanted to go to his lecture, smiling now, his A2 sketches for an eco-apartment tucked under his arm. It seemed that the grief of the morning had passed and he was feeling stronger. We agreed to meet in town later in the day. I had booked the window seat at one of the new bistros on Linnégatan for his birthday lunch, and I watched him walk off over the tarmac towards the department building.

'See you at half twelve?' I shouted.

'*Ja!*' he replied, waving without turning around.

His father drove off, and I walked over to the café in the students' union, where I took a corner table, out of eyeshot of the barista, hoping to sit for the morning and do my work. A few hours went by. Reading my books had taken me somewhere else – the Church of St Francis Xavier in Liverpool, where Hopkins delivered some sermons and tended to the poor – and I was wrapped up in trying to make a connection to his sonnets when my phone began to buzz, moving in an erratic circle on the table. I picked it up to stop the noise. I didn't have the number saved. It was a landline, so I answered with some suspicion, wondering who in Sweden would be calling me.

'Hello?' I said, a questioning tone in my voice, but no one replied. It was totally quiet, and then I heard a murmur, what sounded like a sob, and then a word or two I couldn't make out. 'Hello? Who is it?'

The voice spoke again, indistinctly, and I recognised it: it was Elias. But his voice was distant somehow, strange, as if it were coming from somewhere else, from a place inside himself that I hadn't heard him speak from before.

'Seán?'

The word was slurred, slightly alien and unsettling, as though he were drunk or high.

'Elias?' I said. 'What's wrong? Where are you?'

Again, just a noise, something warbling and uncanny, then a long silence.

'I don't know,' he said.

'What do you mean you don't know?'

My body froze. I felt like a weight had dropped straight through me. The students, the clinks and chatter of the cafeteria, all of it seemed to extend outwards, far away from me, as though a vast space were opening around me. I pushed the table away, knocking my coffee over it and swearing. I threw my books and laptop into my bag, and stumbled in a blur of panic towards the rotating door of the café.

'Elias. Talk to me. Please. Where are you?'

I pictured him far away, a cliff by the sea, a desolate field outside the city. He sounded like a child, his voice lost somewhere, as though it had wandered out of his body.

'Elias, are you there?'

No answer.

I rushed across the courtyard, past the fountain, against the current of students leaving classrooms. Then I heard him again.

He was saying, 'I love you, goodbye, I love you,' and my knees started to give way beneath me.

'No, please, please don't. I'll find you. Where are you? Just tell me, please. I'll come to you. Elias, please.'

I stopped by the main road, the traffic rushing past, not knowing how I'd found myself there, trying to think what else I could say to make him change his mind.

I was so scared, but I couldn't make myself shout. It was as if I were frozen inside myself, or caught in a nightmare where sound didn't exist. I was on a campus full of people, and maybe somewhere deep down I was so afraid of causing a scene that I couldn't raise my voice, even if by raising it, by screaming, I could save him.

'Please,' I whispered, my legs shaking, the phone nearly falling out of my hand. 'Please don't. I'm here, I'm here.'

I began to run along the main road, telling him I would find him, that everything would be OK.

'Just tell me where you are and I'll come to you. It'll all be OK, Elias. Hush now, hush, I'm coming.'

He barely spoke. I was terrified of losing signal or of my battery running out.

I couldn't bring myself to hang up while I called for help, but I knew I had to. I had no car, no way of getting to him. Eventually, I managed to keep him on hold while I called his father. I was petrified that – in the time it would take to make the call – Elias would hang up.

'It's Elias,' I told his father, without saying hello first. 'He's gone somewhere. We need to find him.'

His father must have sensed the panic in my voice.

Perhaps he knew instinctively what I meant, without me having to say it. Either way, he asked me where I was, and then hung up quickly.

'Elias, are you still there?'

There was a long silence, then the sound of his breath, and then a single, quiet word: *'Ja.'*

The next thing I knew his father had left work and sped through the city, bolting two red lights, to pick me up. I saw him pull in to the layby, barely slowing down.

Elias had told me by this point that he was out at the family summerhouse, on a rocky scrap of the archipelago, over an hour away. I had no idea how he had got there. I had no idea what he was doing, or if we'd be able to stop him.

His father and I drove through the city centre as quickly as we could. At Korsvägen, we got stuck as two trams slowed into their stops, blocking the road for what felt like an eternity, the long seconds stretching out like a torture. I watched the people board the tram, piling into the narrow doors, heard the announcements and the hiss as the doors folded back into place. Still, they went nowhere and I bashed my hand against the dashboard of the car in frustration. I checked: Elias was still on the phone.

Finally, with a clang, the bells rang out and the carriages grinded into motion again along the tracks, clearing the way. Then we were off: we joined the motorway from the slip road at speed. All the time, I was speaking to Elias on the phone, trying to keep him on the line, trying to distract him or keep him occupied, bringing up old jokes, telling whatever story came into my head. South America, Liverpool, his friends, whatever might remind him of a time before all of this. I kept trying to, but I couldn't picture him, because I didn't know what he was doing. The sat nav was predicting our time of arrival at nearly an hour away, and each time the minutes decreased on the dashboard I felt a small relief. We were getting closer. We would make it in time, surely.

Then, indicating off the motorway, up on to a round-about, we took a long road through the forest. The deeper we drove, the higher and thicker the fir trees stacked around us, looming over the road until they were almost touching at the top, but for a thin slip of sky. Elias's voice started to cut off, to jar and blur as the signal on my phone began to falter, edging down to zero, where I would lose him. The pines flashed by, blurring into a rapid slide of green. Occasionally, a glint of sunlight on water would shimmer behind them, and then be snatched away by the speed of the car.

'Hello?' Elias's voice, panicking, on the end of the faint line. 'Are you there?'

I replied, over and over, 'Yes, I'm here. I'm here, don't go,' praying that the words would carry over, that he'd hear me, that he'd know I hadn't left him. Then the forest stopped suddenly and we hurtled out into an expanse of green, frosted fields, a burst of sky and light, as if the lid had been lifted off the world.

'Hello?' I said. 'Hello?'

Elias's voice came clear and audible. 'I'm still here.'

When, finally, we drove along the dirt path to the blue cabin, I opened the door before the car had stopped moving and ran down the driveway, across the veranda, and burst open the old, rickety door. Elias was slumped on the couch, away from the window. I didn't know how I expected to find him, but it wasn't like this. He was so defeated, so numb. He looked up very slowly when I walked in, his eyes distant, as though he were trapped behind them. Any familiarity we had managed on the phone call, any of the value of distraction, was gone. He didn't say anything at all. I sat beside him on the long, wooden couch, his head on my lap, stroking his hair, and him too exhausted to move. His father stood quietly by the back door, in shock, perhaps not daring to come closer, not able to look at the scene. I heard the door open as he walked out on to the patio, and felt a sharp salt wind blow into the cabin before the door swung shut with a heavy thud. As I held Elias, I could hear the faint murmur of conversation outside: his father, calling his mother, telling her to come.

Through the big, slanting glass that fronted the wooden cabin, the calm sea was rocking in and out of the tide pools, lifting the red seaweed and swelling around it. The heather and the gorse were shaking a little in the breeze, and the horizon was pink, shooting its last rays up into the clouds and illuminating them from behind. We had swam here often in the summer, dipping down into the glass of the sea and floating for what felt like hours. Now the day was sinking again into night, and we sat in silence as I rocked Elias in my arms, holding his head close to my chest, unable to comprehend how he had found himself here, how all of this was happening.

After half an hour, his mother arrived. She worked in a town close by and had left work abruptly, forgetting to offer an explanation. She came into the cabin, looking frail and panicked. I didn't know what Elias's father had told her, or even exactly what he knew, but clearly the two of them were, like me, in shock. She was small, with cropped grey hair and big green eyes that opened widely behind her square glasses, and when she came over to us, she hardly spoke, her head bowed and timid.

'*Hej, Elias, älskling, det är mamma.*'

He looked up to her, and in his face she saw something that told her that words were useless, that this was beyond their capacity to help. And so she sat by his side, stroking his arm, shaking her head sadly and looking at her son.

Elias barely said a word. After a while, his mother nodded to me, and then stood up and went to sit by the table, where Elias's father now was. When he knew that his parents were on the far side of the room, out of hearing, Elias pulled my ear close to his mouth, and whispered something to me. I couldn't make it out at first, but he was repeating the same phrase over and over.

'I was so close, Seán. I was going to do it. I was so close.'

His blue jeans were scuffed and his forehead was hot. I brushed his hair with my fingers, stroking it, hushing as I held him. Then, on the table, right by his parents, I saw a bottle of white rum standing with its lid off, and beside it a mess of papers and packing. Elias followed my gaze, and when he saw what I was looking at, he clasped on to me. My eyes were wide with horror. He looked straight into them with a terrifying desperation, as though he didn't know what he was more afraid of: the world or himself.

From that moment, I came to know that fear exactly, though from an entirely different perspective. For the weeks that followed, I would be afraid of Elias, as though he was a new person now, or was inhabited by a new person; someone who might, at any moment, kill him. It was as though he was shadowed at every turn by an inversion of himself, someone who stalked his every thought and followed his every move, and whispered dark things in his ear. He was both the man I loved and the person who wanted to kill the man I loved. And as time went by, I would be afraid of myself, afraid that the stalking stranger had turned his eyes on me and was, slowly, silently, inhabiting me, too.

It was only later that day that I found out what had happened. After we had taken him to university that morning, the morning of his birthday, Elias had skipped lectures and taken two buses and a train to get to the summerhouse. He had planned the whole thing. It turned out that he had never answered the phone to the doctor. He had faked the conversation when he thought I might be listening. Instead, he had gone into the downstairs bathroom, opened the cupboard and stashed all the tablets he could find into his rucksack. After he said goodbye in the car park, smiling as he walked off, he turned a corner and ran. All the way – on the backseats of buses and the carriages of the trains, seeing the city unravel into forest, then into farmland, and finally the coast – he knew exactly what he wanted to do.

*

After Elias had fallen asleep, exhausted, empty, I covered him with an old felt blanket, drew the blinds, and went out on to the lawn behind the house. His parents were sitting at the kitchen table, in silence, and the cabin felt stifling. My mind was a frenzied, living thing, whirring against the cage of my skull. The summerhouse was no longer just a summerhouse, but a place where something, some world-changing thing, had happened. It was the centre of the new world I had been carried into. The clocks had re-set. Everything started again here.

Outside, the cold was biting, but the sea air started to calm the panic in my head. The lawn was stitched all over with plantain and the dried bodies of wildflowers, and was overgrown around the edges with a rust of bracken. The

wild lupins that grew here in summer were all shrunken
back to the tuber, and only a wick of pink light was cooling
over the sea. I closed my eyes, pressed my lips to the cold
air, and balanced myself against it, as though I were lowering myself slowly into a new reality. Out here in June,
before a party, we had been cutting back the lupins and they
seemed miraculous to me, so profuse and wild – their
upright, electric-blue spears – as if the flowers held all the
energy of the sky and the dimming night. Later in the summer, Elias had given me some seeds to take home to my
mother. And here I was, standing by them, in an entirely
different world. I listened to the tide and felt myself swaying, as if the waters in my ear were being lifted. When I
opened my eyes I could almost picture the ghosts of those
lupins gathered around me; luminous, shadowy, standing in
their tall circle, tolling their silent bells.

It is hard to account for the trauma of a thing that didn't
happen, hard to accommodate a fear based in an almost-
event, a thing that might have occurred, but didn't. The
truth, though, is that Elias found himself so close to the
edge of life, came so near to the brink of it, that he changed
us both forever. Still, years later, it is the music of what
almost happened that haunts me most, and will not leave
my mind.

*

Later, back in the suburb where his parents lived, we put
Elias to bed. In the morning, we would take him to the hospital, but for now, he needed sleep. He went easily, lying
down fully clothed under the covers, curled on his side,
quiet and in shock. I left his parents to keep watch, unlatched

the front door of the house and walked out on to the silent, moonlit road, down to the lake, stopping at a late-night supermarket to buy a packet of cigarettes and a lighter. I didn't usually smoke, but I needed it then – the fuzzing warmth in my head, the deep, momentary inhalation. The cigarette, once I lit it, kept my mind occupied on something slow and repetitive.

It was a clear night and the stars were out in force, spread over the black sky. I heard Hopkins's voice in my mind: 'The fields of heaven covered with eye-brights.' And then, again: 'Night's lantern / Pointed with piercèd lights.' Scraps of poems floating around, even now, and they were useless. I couldn't see flowers in the stars, or a lantern in the night; just a cold, unforgiving openness, an endless depth of dark above me. There was no consolation in the world, no beauty in its mute gaze.

It was past eleven o'clock, and I braved myself to call my mother, to tell her what had happened. When she answered the phone and I heard her voice, this time it was me who couldn't speak. She heard me and knew that something was wrong, and when she asked what it was, the whole flood of the day came crashing through me and I let out an unearthly, animal sound. The cry seemed to drag itself out of me. It didn't feel like it belonged to my body at all. I dropped my cigarette on the ground and began to sob, barely able to hold the phone to my ear. I might have woken half the street, but I didn't care. The shock that had been holding me together finally gave way.

In my mind a new universe of possibilities I had never considered before reeled and span open like black holes. Gradually, through halted breaths, I told her what had happened. I hadn't yet found the time or the courage to tell

Elias's parents about the tablets, the bottle of rum open on the table. I wasn't sure that they knew the full extent of what had been avoided. At the end of our call, after I had calmed down enough to listen to reason, my mother pressed me.

'You have to tell them,' she said. 'What if he does it again?'

I knew she was right. I sat by the lake and smoked a few more cigarettes, one after the other until my throat was sore. How would I do it? How would I find the words? I tried to calm myself by looking out on the black water, the moon's pathway rippling over the surface, the tiny wavelets tipping their light against the shore.

When I got back to the house, all the windows were dark except for the long rectangle of the kitchen, where I could see Elias's father sitting in silence at the dining table. I walked up the steep pathway to the front door and opened it. Before I went to the kitchen, I opened the door to Elias's room. He was asleep, still fully clothed under the covers, totally still. I closed the door gently and stood in the hallway, taking one deep breath after another. I slipped off my shoes, and went through to speak to his father. I was fearful, and didn't know how he would react. If he made the same sound that I had, that animal cry, how could I bear it?

When I went into the kitchen he looked up, his eyes sore and red, a glass of tepid water on the table in front of him.

'I need to tell you something,' I said, sitting down opposite him.

I took a shaky breath and repeated, as best as I could, what Elias had told me: the bottle of rum he had taken from the garage, the tablets he had packed into his bag, how he had sat at the dining table in the summerhouse, pressed each pill out of its white tray, and gathered them all into small handfuls. How he had made a list of people to call. There was an order, and I realised on repeating it that it must have been difficult for his father to hear. First, there was me, then his brothers, then finally his mother and his father. Perhaps I was the easiest; or perhaps Elias hoped I would stop him before he could go any further. Either way, he had picked up the phone and, after a few rings, I had answered.

Elias's father cried quietly as I told him this, shaking his head, unable to process it. But as I pieced together the narrative aloud, a new terror dawned on me.

Where were the tablets now?

They hadn't been on the table with the empty packets and the rum.

Where were they?

Without finishing my sentence, I pushed my chair with a screech away from the table and ran into the hallway, slipping on the varnished wood. I saw Elias's bag, slung by the door. I grabbed it and pulled it open. Elias's father had run after me and let out a howl when he saw what was inside the bag. It was stuffed full of pill packets – paracetamol, ibuprofen, antihistamines, antibiotics, tablets for nausea, laxatives, antidiarrheals – everything Elias could find in the bathroom cupboard. As I reached down and pulled out the packets, the bag seemed bottomless. More and more and more. I threw them across the hallway. Half the packets were emptied, but the pills were gone. Had he taken them already? Had he lied to me?

I thought of Elias, totally still and silent on the bed, and I scrambled, pulled open his bedroom door and shook him violently awake.

'Where are they? Elias! Wake up! Where are they? Where are they? Where are they?'

He didn't speak. He barely opened his eyes, but he knew what I was asking. With hardly any expression on his face, he moved his hands slowly downwards, and turned out his trouser pockets. Each was stuffed full of pills, all shapes and colours, hundreds of them, spilling out on to the bedsheets. His front pockets, then his back pockets – fists and fists of them.

*

When Elias and I had lived together in Liverpool – that year before we moved to Gothenburg – we would often walk down to the docks after work in the evening. It was always windy, sometimes buffeting about our heads like a mania, dragging our feet from under us. Other times there was just a light salt-breeze, lifting the fret up off the Mersey and over the quayside walls. Down by the river, on the side of the old docks, inscriptions in roman numerals recorded the tide. You could see them if you stood on the dock wall and leant over it, looking down into the choppy swell of the river. Averaging out the still-water level, the gauge had once been used as the standard for measuring altitude by the Ordnance Survey. Ten metres above sea-level, anywhere in the world, meant ten metres above the measure recorded on this stone wall, just down the road from our flat.

At the top of the meter, close to where our feet were, the numerals read twenty-four, and then descended in increments down to the water. When the river was low enough, and had receded to the point that the silt would dry up and smell, and the gulls would swoop to pick out the flecks of eels in the bed, you could see right down to the bottom. As the tide lowered, the numerals were revealed, right down to the carved 'I' – the number one – at the foot of the measure. Elias used to come down to see it often. He would marvel at it, thinking that this, here, was the very foot of it, the place against which the height of all the hills and mountains and moors in the world had been quantified. The imperial city had made itself the measurement of the world it sought to conquer. When we were in Popayán, Elias found, we were nearly 2,000 metres above this point. That time we got altitude sickness in La Paz, we were more than 3,500 metres above it.

When Elias took himself to the summerhouse that day, it felt as though a new depth gauge had been set, a new numeral against which everything else would be measured. The point of suicide, the brink of it, was inscribed, and recalibrated our world. It became the arbiter of all joy and sadness. Everything from now on was judged on its proximity to that lowest numeral. When Elias was sad and wouldn't get out of bed, I would try desperately to define how far from the light he was, what depth he had attained.

Elias was all that I could cling to. My happiness was no longer my own, but his. My dark days were his dark days. For almost a year after his birthday, I waited anxiously for any sign that the tide was turning, but on and on the waves kept tumbling in, knocking us under. I gripped my phone in my hand everywhere I went. I slept with it in my hand, turned it off silent, fearing more than anything that I would miss a call, would miss the moment when everything repeated and I was not there to stop it. I could hardly bear to sleep at first, terrified of not being awake, of not being alert. Then, as time went by, it wasn't just a phone call from Elias that I dreaded. I began to think that everyone would call me, everyone I loved, and every call would be their last.

On that first night, after we had flushed the tablets down the toilet, his mother slept on the floor in the doorway, so that if he tried to leave while we were sleeping she would wake up. We effectively barricaded him in, not knowing what else to do. Lying next to him in the downstairs room, reeling through a new world of possible endings, I thought back to the start of the day, when everything was wrong, but I hadn't known it. It was a bright morning and I had got up early, quietly slipping out of the bed and into the kitchen. I walked with a cake lit with candles down the wooden corridor and into the bedroom, and sang to Elias in bed as he woke, trying to coax a smile, some sign that he was happy to be lifted out of sleep and into the world again. All I can picture now is his face glowing in the light, his deep, haunted eyes, and the Swedish happy birthday song I sang to him in a quiet whisper as the sun drifted through the blinds, *Ja, må han leva! Ja, må han leva! Ja, må han leva uti hundrade år!* I rolled my *r*'s as I sang. *Yes, may he live, Yes, may he live, Yes, may he live for a hundred years.*

*

The next day – after a disturbed night of almost-sleep – before Elias woke, I got up and sat by the desk. The two mornings seemed to belong to two different lives. As the sun rose, the trees broke with spears of light. It was perverse to sit there, I thought, and watch the world outside beginning to wake – the doors of the garages lifting up and sliding back; the neighbours readying their kids for school; everything carrying on as before when so much had changed. As Elias slept behind me, I noticed something on the painted surface of the desk, something strange, only showing itself now because of the way the morning had pried its way into the room. It was Elias's name, written in capital letters, with the rubber end of a pencil, so that the word was spelled out in the marking of the eraser on the white gloss veneer. *E-L-I-A-S.*

I ran my finger along it, feeling its rough, raised shape. *E-L-I-A-S.* His name, uncovered there like an artefact, a part of him revealed. The writing was a hybrid of doing and undoing, an inscription that, in being inscribed, was also a sort of vanishing. I turned back to see him still asleep, still fully dressed in yesterday's clothes, and I imagined him sitting here at the desk where I was sitting, one day, perhaps even yesterday, before we left the house, taking out the pencil and making his mark, some word to say *I am here.* Strange, but beautiful, too – to write his name with an eraser, with the white squeak of the rubber against the desk, perhaps when he least felt its presence, least felt the utility of something that marked his place in the world. His name, something pale and personal – as though he, too, had sat there, thinking about what it was he had been given, and trying to make sense of it by writing it down.

IV

That morning, the GP referred Elias to a hospital in a town on the far border of the municipality, over an hour's car journey from home. Leaving the suburb meant taking a thin road that tailed through the pine forest. As we drove deeper, the green woods gloomed around us, the tall, dark trees standing in high ranks at each side of the road, like some ancient army watching us carrying the wounded to safety. We stayed quiet for most of the journey – Elias sleeping in the back next to me, or just closing his eyes, shutting out the endless stream of the woods blurring beyond the window. He hardly spoke, but when he did, he slurred slightly, and his voice had a warbling, exhausted thinness. My eyes were tight and sore, and I leant myself against the shuddering window of the car. Trees, trees, trees, and the rhythmic thud of the road. The world outside was on fast forward, as though time was moving past us out there, leaving us behind. When we hurtled out of the forest and into the yellow farmland, rooks lifted over the open fields. Everything was silent, but it was a ringing silence that seemed to pierce right through me. It felt as though my body had been struck, like a tuning fork, held to some alien frequency. Roads, trees, fields, birds. The world was there and somehow we were not.

When we reached the hospital, we parked under a row of maples, their leaves crisp and reddening, their fire slowly burning through to the stem. I opened the door for Elias and he clambered out, moving as though his body were too heavy for him to manage. I kept my head down; afraid, I think, of being seen, of being witnessed. Outside the main lobby a few outdoor tables were strewn in the autumn sun – there were leftover coffee cups, a newspaper, two nurses smoking by the rotating door. Inside, the fresh air was replaced with the ominous smell of the hospital – antiseptic, bleach – everything but the scent of bodies purged away. The receptionist gestured us to wait in a small consulting room, where Elias sat on a plastic-covered bed, his head still bowed, like a prisoner awaiting a sentence. His mother and father took two chairs by a round green coffee table, and I sat on the narrow windowsill, feeling myself set apart from the family unit. A cold draught blew through the old seal around the glass. There were voices outside, but they were dim, the words inaudible. A black crow was tearing apart a foil wrapper, shaking it with its head. It flapped in the dead leaves, which lifted and then fell, briefly animated.

It wasn't long before there was a light rap on the door. A psychiatric consultant came into the room, a clipboard in her hand, and introduced herself. She asked a few routine questions (name, address, date of birth), but Elias did not speak. He barely raised his head. When I moved to help, about to answer her inquiries for him, she raised her hand gently. I nodded, apologetically, and leant back against the glass. After a few moments, the vacuum of the silence became so heavy that Elias raised his head finally, his eyes meeting hers.

'Hello, Elias,' she said, kindly.

No reaction. Then, quietly, he gave a murmured 'Hello.'

She returned it with an encouraging smile, a slow nod. 'Why do you think you're here?'

I couldn't bear to look at his face. I wanted to take his hand, to let him know I was with him.

Slowly, he began to speak, very quietly, murmuring and hesitant at first, his eyes fixed to the floor under his feet, his hands turning over each other, squeezing and loosening. Then, for the first time, he did what he would have to do over and over in the coming weeks: narrate the story of his birthday, what he had done and why he had done it. The consultant offered a sympathetic silence, the occasional encouraging nod, until his story arrived at the present moment, at the four of us, sitting dumbstruck in a psychiatric ward. It didn't seem possible that it had all happened in less than a day. I could not recall the person I was on the morning of the day before. That person had no idea what was coming. He was unrecognisable to me now.

After Elias was done, the consultant asked a few more questions, checking details, repeating certain phrases, making sure she understood. Then, as gently as she had arrived, she left us. As she walked out of the room, the silence descended again over us. We were taken to an adjoining ward where the main doors locked electronically, so that only the staff could let anyone enter or leave. A doctor lifted her key-card to the black box by the doorframe: the light switched green and the lock clunked open. Inside, there was a main corridor, a few consulting rooms to our right, numbered bedrooms along the left, and at the end a dining room with a hatch canteen, a few sofas, a TV playing on mute.

At the main door we were met by two nurses. They spoke softly but authoritatively in Swedish, addressing us, but their words came too quickly for me to process. They saw my confusion and pointed to a laminated poster on the wall of the corridor. Did we have anything on us that might be sharp? Did we have any pills, any cigarette lighters, any strings or cables? Any knives, any scissors, any solvents? There was a locked closet, we learned, where they kept the contraband. We searched our pockets and patted them innocently to show they were empty. Already I felt like I had mistakenly stepped out of line. They led us along the corridor to room No. 10, which was to be Elias's room, and out of nowhere I blurted out, 'My shoes!'

They looked at me, not understanding.

'Sorry, ummm, my shoes, they have laces.' I pointed down to them, as though to prove it. 'Is that . . . are they OK?'

Yes, shoelaces were fine, they said, just so long as I didn't leave the shoes lying around.

We went inside the bedroom. At first it appeared normal, if bare. A small single bed, an armchair, an adjoining laminate bathroom. Elias sat on the bed, then lay down, closing his eyes. As I sat in the armchair, leaving him to rest, I began to notice small absences, small precautions. The bins, for a start, didn't have bags. The window blinds were behind security glazing and had no cord. There was no table lamp by the bed; nothing to soften the almost constant glare of the overhead lighting. Anything that might be used to hurt oneself was gone: doorknobs, rounded hinges, towel-bars. All the furniture was weighted down. Later, I learned that this was to stop patients from barricading themselves into their rooms. My eyes darted around, and I began to see in what wasn't there, in the absences, a sort of dark inversion of a room, an inventory of all the ways a person might harm themselves, a key to all the vulnerabilities of the body. The slit wrist, the ruptured throat, and those ways beyond any I could have imagined before. Doorknobs, plastic bags, table lamps, shoelaces: my mind raced through images, a litany of violence, of possible futures, possible endings. I held my hands close to my face, as though I might betray myself. I was there for support, not for panic. As Elias rested, and his parents went to speak to the doctor, I stood up, walked to the window and stared out of it at the cars in the car park, the families, the buses arriving and departing, and I thought how impossible it was that Elias and I could go out into that world again. Behind me, voices drifted in from the corridor: nurses, patients, a woman screaming for her son, another crying that all her teeth were missing. I pushed my forehead against the cold glass and closed my eyes.

During that first day there was a long schedule of meetings: nurses, doctors, a medication review, a treatment plan. Nothing set in stone, no promises. When I spoke to the consultant alone, I wanted to know what had happened and how it would be fixed. A chemical imbalance set right; a trauma healed; a definite cause with a definite solution. The mind, I learned, was not quite so amenable as that. Meanwhile, Elias's father drove back to the house to get a bag of things – clothes, a book, the laptop. His mother went out to the shop to buy anything she could think of that Elias might eat. Most of the day I spent sitting next to him on his bed, mostly in silence, watching daytime TV. Occasionally, I would reach out to touch him, but he was stony and unmoving, his body almost uninhabited, his mind elsewhere.

We watched hours of reruns of the same Swedish game-show. The contestants had to guess what city they were in by watching a video of a train approaching a station. Clues in the landscape, the occasional road sign, the architecture. Each was quickly apprehended, until someone pressed a buzzer and shouted *Munich!* or *Barcelona!* or *Tallinn!* The train would start off miles outside the city, and the quicker the answer was called, the more points were won. Elias had been everywhere, and loved to travel. Eventually, with a sort of reluctant mumble, he started to guess along. He was disarmingly good at it, and it gave me hope to see his eyes moving across the screen, invested. Mostly, I just spluttered wrong answers or gave up too soon. Sometimes one of the contestants would guess it almost straight away, when all I could see was a bare track stretching into the distance. And then there were the occasional rounds where the train would start off along the tracks, the video streaming: the trees flashing to open fields, then slowly the greenery would thin out and there were houses, then high-rises, then the station approaching, and the whole panel of contestants would sit, flustered, confused, and still none of them could guess where it was they had arrived.

*

I wanted to stay overnight, to sleep in the armchair by his bed. It was against the rules, but I couldn't bear to leave Elias alone in that strange empty room, staring into space. All those noises – the buzzers, the doors, the hushed conversations in the corridor. I stayed way past visiting hours, but the nurses were kind and said they didn't mind, so long as we kept inside the room. Eventually, after he had fallen asleep, and I was struggling to keep my sore eyes open, I kissed him on his forehead and held his hand and said goodbye. His father arrived to collect me, and we left and drove the long route back home, where I slept a broken, shallow sleep in Elias's childhood bed.

The next day I woke up before 5 a.m. with a dull headache, my jaw aching. It was pitch-dark outside, the ground hard and frozen, an almost total silence in the street. I couldn't believe I'd left Elias alone for the whole night. I needed to get back to him. I needed to know that he was all right. He felt so far away. I pictured him waking alone in that room, and I couldn't bear it. For the first few days, we drove out to the hospital to be with him, sitting around his bed, trying to distract him, to convince him of the goodness of the world, when we least believed in it ourselves. After half a week, the nurses took us quietly to one side and said that so many visitors wasn't always a good idea, and that Elias needed time alone, to process, to come to terms with himself.

Every day I would wake up in the empty house. Elias's parents went to work early, but they would leave eggs on the sideboard for me, or a few cinnamon buns on a plate. I could never figure out the coffee machine, so I boiled water in a saucepan and used a filter, pouring the strong coffee into my cup and throwing away the grounds. Most mornings I'd sit out on the front doorstep with my coffee, wearing my winter coat and smoking cigarettes, trying to clear the tension in my head. Then I'd go back inside, into the downstairs room, and do some work, trying my best to write a few pages of my thesis, to not fall behind or raise suspicion at the university. After the grey light had started to rise in the street, I would pack up my books into my bag and walk into the town centre to take the 10 a.m. train. After that, there was an hour-long bus from Alingsås, then a forty-minute walk through the next town and up to the hospital. Every day the same long journey, even if only to sit by Elias during the afternoons, to work quietly in the corner of his room while he watched TV, to be beside him.

My days, over the four weeks Elias spent in the hospital, had variations – small smiles from passengers who travelled the same route at the same times; a kind word from the man in the newsagent where I bought my coffee. For Elias, though, the boredom was absolute. In the ward there was a small interior garden, though it didn't get much sun, especially at this time of year, and besides it was too cold to sit out for more than ten minutes at a time. The food was served like clockwork at lunch and dinnertime in the same small portions. There were no flowers, no plants. Nothing grew, nothing bloomed. Only a few sickly Monet prints lined the mint-green walls. Otherwise, he had his book, the endless daytime TV, a few fellow patients who came closer, intrigued by a young, handsome man in their midst. It turned out that the older woman I had heard shouting on that first day would take out her dentures, then cry, inconsolably, that she had no teeth. There was a man who told me every day that his son was going to visit, but he never did. Once, when I arrived on the ward and went into the lounge, he looked up at me and broke into a smile. 'Finally!' he said, in Swedish. 'I knew you'd come.'

As the days passed, Elias began to be scared that his fate was with these people, that he was one of them, after all. I started to notice that he had changed. There was some glint in his eye that made me nervous, and he had a newfound darkness to his humour. There was a blade behind it. He had always teased me, and I had liked it, but now he seemed serious. Sometimes he was taunting and savage, and I couldn't bear it, and pleaded with him to stop. Once he told me that he had explained to the doctor about the pills, the rum, and she had told him that a death like that, even if it came, was not instantaneous and was deeply unpleasant.

'Not a good idea,' she said. 'Kidney failure, coma, brain damage.'

He told me he had asked her for other ways, better ways, and she had stared at him sternly, straight in the eyes, and said, 'I'm not giving you tips.'

He smiled as he told me that, and looked at me as though he wanted me to laugh along with him. Really, I didn't know what he wanted. It was as if he were testing the waters to see what he could get away with. To me, it felt like a warning, a caution not to let my guard down. The worst, he seemed to be saying, was yet to come.

Over those weeks it felt as though Elias treated our relationship as something to be tested, a boundary to be pushed. I think he wanted to see me fight for it, for him. How long would I put up with him? How far would I follow him? To what lengths would I go to save him? He was convinced I would get bored eventually, that I would leave him to it. He was convinced that I was better off without him, and he was waiting for me to realise it too. If I was too slow, too patient, he seemed to say, he would push further, push harder, until I broke, until I proved him right.

Because of this, because I knew I was being tested, I was scared to leave him alone. On my bus journeys back to his parents' house, I couldn't shake that stalking stranger from my mind. I felt a sickening fear every time my phone rang, as though Elias was being held hostage, and this time, this time, it was over. Once I took him a Fleetwood Mac CD to listen to, and remembered on the bus home that I'd left it in his room. I couldn't sleep. All night I drifted off, then woke in panics as if I were falling through the bed. I saw him breaking the disc into shards, cutting his wrists, the pool of blood seeping under the door into the corridor of the ward.

Alarms. Nurses running. My fault. My fault. The next day I sprinted to the hospital as soon as the bus stopped, and rushed into his room. The CD, untouched, was exactly where I'd left it and I cried with relief. Elias stared at me, perplexed, wondering what was going on.

This went on and on and became, eerily, normal. A fortnight in, Elias seemed to be slightly improved, and he was given a review with the consultant, who asked him if he thought he could be trusted to go outside unaccompanied, once a day or so, for a walk. He told them he thought he could, and I was terrified. My trust was shattered. I couldn't bear to let him be alone with himself, unwatched. Wasn't it just another clever trick, the underhanded calculation of a way out? All I could think of was those absences in the room, and their corresponding presences outside: blades, wires, trees. Then, outwards: pharmacies, rivers, train tracks, the motorway. It was endless. Once he was out there, how could I keep him safe?

We sat in his room – me on the armchair, him on the edge of the bed – and I took hold of both his hands and looked directly into his eyes.

'Be honest with me, Elias. Please. If I had a gun here,' I said, 'and I gave it to you, would you do it?'

Without hesitation, the answer came. He smiled.

'Yes'.

*

Everything, those weeks, was uncanny. My imagination was parasitic, exhausting me before I'd even woken up, burning through my body. My writing – and the books I was reading in the scraps of time on journeys between home and hospital – seemed to merge in and out of real life; the boundaries blurring between Hopkins's work and the life I was in. Every day I would get the train and the bus, sometimes through the steely dark of early morning, mostly through sleet and rain. And every day, speeding past the soaking pinewoods, the trees all huddled in their wet shawls, I would take out my book and try my best to read as the carriages shuddered or the buses rounded their corners. Hopkins and myself, somehow brought into tandem, meeting and parting like two currents in a long river.

Years ago I had fallen in love with the strange rhythms of his poems: they were like complex, many-sided jewels you could turn over and over, always seeing a new flash of meaning. Then, poem by poem, I found that I had fallen in love, in a way, with Hopkins himself, desiring him over the breach of a century. Friends described his nervous grace. He was effeminate and fearless. I saw him enchanted by the inscapes of bluebells, studying the crystals in frozen mud, weeping over the felling of a tree. Once, I read, when he was training as a Jesuit in Lancashire, in the north of England, one of the old Fathers pointed him out to a gardener.

'That man is a great scholar,' he said.

The gardener didn't believe him. 'I saw him the other day in the garden turning round and round and looking at a piece of glass on the path. I took him for a natural [a child, an idiot].'

I loved that Hopkins was so quiet, so acute, so original.

'All things therefore,' he wrote in one of his sermons, 'are charged with love, are charged with God and if we knew how to touch them give off sparks and take fire, yield drops and flow, ring and tell of him.'

The world, after I read that, was a different place altogether.

Guiltily, though, I realised now that I had also loved the tragedy of him. He was burnt out by life, and all the while he was offering me the glowing embers of his thought, lighting a way. When he died, aged forty-four, his death notice read that 'He had a most subtle mind, which too quickly wore out the fragile strength of his body.' Perhaps that was what I was drawn to: the fact that it was love for the world that tortured him. I thought I knew what that was like. But now, in the blur of another's breakdown, I saw it all differently. Reading through his poems, from the ecstatic early verse to the final, dark sonnets, it was hard to tell where exactly the lights went out. It felt like watching a gradual, sweeping desolation.

When he moved to Dublin, in the last years of his short life, he wrote a series of sonnets that were disorientating and painful to read. He writhed, sweated, panicked, called out for comfort and found none. He was a 'wretch' in darkness, wrestling with God, 'this tormented mind / With this tormented mind tormenting yet.' Even the syntax was tortuous. In one of the poems, he called himself a 'lonely began', making a noun of his incompletion, his desperate sense of having no future. Now, it felt like he was remonstrating me again; not, this time, for being indoors or for not looking at the stars, but for presuming that I could ever know him.

> O the mind, mind has mountains; cliffs of fall
> Frightful, sheer, no-man-fathomed. Hold them cheap
> May who ne'er hung there.

That impassable, treacherous terrain of the mind, those chasms of despair. How could anyone who hadn't felt those cliffs know them? How could I ever know Hopkins, or Elias? How could I ever see past the mirrored surface that reflected everything back at me with my own image imposed across it? But maybe that mirror was what I needed. There was something he was showing me, a line where empathising with another meant empathising with myself, too. Hopkins wrote that 'What you look hard at seems to look hard at you.' And so here we were, looking hard at each other, and I was puzzling him for clues.

On one of those bus journeys to visit Elias, I put aside the poems and read Hopkins's journals instead, and knew I was reading something that wasn't meant to be read. Still, I couldn't shake the sense that it was myself I was reading, or that I was projecting myself and Elias back over 150 years of history. At Oxford, Hopkins had fallen in love with a fellow poet, Digby Dolben. He shared Hopkins's fascination with High Church ritual – incense and gowns and flagellation – and they plotted in secret to convert to Catholicism. But love, rather than elating Hopkins, terrified him. Digby Dolben was nineteen years old when he died. He drowned in a river, carrying a boy on his chest, trying to save the child from sinking under the water. Hopkins only heard about his death a month later, when he arrived to find a letter waiting for him. In his journal he wrote, 'See June 28.' That was the day Dolben had died, and Hopkins seemed to be forcing a comparison between all the things he had been doing on that day, unknowingly, as somewhere miles away his lover drowned. When Hopkins heard the news, he wrote to a friend:

There is very little I have to say. I looked forward to meeting Dolben and his being a Catholic more than to anything. At the same time from never having met him but once I find it difficult to realise his death or feel as if it were anything to me. You know there can very seldom have happened the loss of so much beauty (in body and mind and life) and the promise of still more as there has been in his case – seldom, I mean, in the whole world.

Hopkins told a friend that, someday, 'I hope to see Finedon and the place where he was drowned.' Dolben's body was interred in the family vault beneath the altar of Finedon Church. And although Hopkins told his friend that he met Dolben 'but once', he met him over and over in the freedom of his dreams.

Still, each imagined meeting was stitched with guilt and apprehension. There were moments of dark humour in the obvious shame of the journals – Hopkins noting down each time he ejaculated, whether involuntarily or not, with the regret-filled abbreviation 'O.H.', for 'Old Habits'. And then there were entries where Hopkins policed himself, almost every day, out of sheer terror at what his body was doing, at what he couldn't stop himself from wanting. I could see him purging himself out of existence.

On 4 December 1867 he felt 'Physical danger while having my arm in Baillie's and speaking affectionately.' Later, 'evil thoughts, especially from Rover lying on me.' I drew a shaky pencil line under the text, and for a split-second pictured Jack and I, sitting up on the apple boughs, the line of a poem set to music. Then, Hopkins again: 'O.H. Temptation. Going on into a letter to Dolben at night against warning.' 'O.H. thrice. Temptations. [...] Losing time. [...] Self-indulgence at own wine. Inattention at chapel.

Desire to be thought better than I am.' 'Running on in thought last night unseasonably against warning on to subject of Dolben, and today and some temptation.'

I read those journals and felt a deep affection, a kinship. Temptation, yes, and the fear of it. What would giving in to it mean? His eyes lingered too long on choirboys. He scared himself into a deep, unshaking fear whenever a boy touched him. Worst, he caught himself transferring his desire on to the muscular body of Christ on the crucifix. But if Hopkins was right, and he met Dolben only once, what an impression the man must have made. Turning through the journals as the bus juddered down the wet roads, reading those lists of sins, the names of men listed and crossed out, it was Dolben who came up repeatedly. There were facsimiles of the manuscripts in the book, and on the opposite page to an entry about Dolben, Hopkins had drafted a poem. It seemed to be about Christ, but really, I wondered, what if Dolben was Christ, or overlaid with Christ, so the obsession with both men became one?

'Let me be to Thee as the circling bird,' Hopkins wrote.

I have found the dominant of my range and state—
Love, O my God, to call Thee Love and Love.

When he was training for the priesthood, Hopkins showed a startling aptitude for self-punishment. He wore a penitential girdle, a metal clamp that he tightened around the top of his leg, the pain distracting him from any stray thoughts. The spikes stuck into his thigh, which made him limp as he walked. He castigated himself, punished himself. Earlier, Dolben had joined him, too, whipping his own back with such ferocity that Hopkins was breathtaken by the sound of the lash. I looked up from my book, out of the window of the bus, streaming with a sleet-rain, and could hear the sound of the lash myself, winced at it, saw the markings it made, the ridges of the scars, and my mind ran on to Elias, sitting alone in his room. In the rush of the speeding vehicle, in the blur of the nightmare, my mind fused myself and Hopkins together. It was as though I had reached back through time and felt a familiar hand, reaching back. Exclusion, difference, impossibility. Maybe there were clues there, after all. Maybe Hopkins had left a code in the poems, or maybe his life could teach me something.

When I arrived at the ward, I hardly remembered getting off the bus or walking through the town, but my jeans were soaked with the rain and I was shaking with the cold. I laughed it off when the nurse looked me up and down and smiled as she gestured me inside.

'Here for Elias?' she asked.

'*Varje dag*,' I answered. 'Every day.'

It had been three weeks now, and when I went into his room I found it empty, and walked further along the corridor, seeing him sitting on the edge of a two-seat sofa in the common area. The television was on mute, but he was watching it anyway, listlessly, as though his mind were elsewhere, too. I said hello, quietly, and placed my hand on his shoulder, not wanting to startle him, but he hardly moved, which told me he knew it was me. He leant his head to one side, so his hair brushed the back of my hand, and I squeezed his shoulder, asking him how he was.

He murmured. 'Fine.'

We went back to his room and he told me some of the things he'd heard from the other patients, how he was scared he'd become like them if he didn't leave soon. One woman kept mistaking him for her husband, telling him things he shouldn't know.

After all these talks with doctors, therapists, nurses, I wondered if anyone had asked him about the root of everything. He'd told them that he was scared he'd never be happy, would never have a family or a career, that everyone he loved would leave him once they knew who he really was. And I asked him, 'Who is it that you really are? What is it you're afraid we'll find out?'

He couldn't say.

'I'm boring,' he suggested, but I knew that didn't cover it.

Part of me wondered if a lifetime of hiding who he really was had left a latent fear of being found out. I was suspicious, though. Was I just coding my own anxieties on to him? Was I listening to him or to myself? I felt my own sense of self shaking in his presence. Just by being there with him, I was coming undone.

'What you look hard at,' I thought, 'seems to look hard at you.'

It had always been like this, Elias said, even in school, even as a child. All he could articulate, at that stage, was an ominous sense that set in very young, an early knowledge that the future wasn't a place he could live, that of all the worlds he could see around him, none seemed made so that he could be happy in them. He would be found out, exposed, and everyone would leave. And I nodded and, despite myself, I felt my own wounds smarting, too, because I knew exactly what he meant, and I felt again a sense of brotherhood with him, this man I loved, who grew up in a different country, with a different language, but had felt the same tenor of dread in childhood that I had too.

*

Not long ago I was on a long drive with my mother, heading north along the west coast to the Lake District and, through stretches of easy silence and the candour that comes through hours of simple conversation, the road providing the odd distraction from any tension, she asked me if I'd been happy as a child. Immediately, I answered yes. And it was true – I was happy, for the most part, very happy. But that happiness was never absolute, because I knew it would be finite. I knew, from the earliest age I can remember, that one day I would have to tell my parents and my friends a secret about myself, a secret I could not escape, and they would leave me, or I would have to leave them, and then my happiness would be over. And so I savoured the happiness, cradled it, saw my childhood (even as I was living it) through a lens of nostalgia. Soon, I knew, it would be over. Soon I would have to end it. There was happiness, yes, but there was always the relentless knowledge of time running out. Love, comfort, safety, all of them ran like sand through an hourglass.

And I wondered, as we drove north and the foothills rose unevenly into mountains, how I had known that, or what had made me think it. How did that fear install itself in me? I was only a child, but still, lodged in my mind was the shrapnel of overheard conversations, innumerable quiet warnings. I was warned about who to play with, who to like, what to like. The television told me. Children at school told me. I remember being shouted at by a friend's mother after I kissed her son. I could only have been seven or eight years old.

'That's dirty,' she said. I can still hear her accent, the way she said *dirrrty*.

What I knew then, instinctively, was that I was dirty, that I was perverse. The more I tried to explain to my mother, the more memories seemed to unearth themselves, like gun-metal from an old field.

Growing up, I veered one way, then the other. I leant, as a child would, into the arms of its protectors. I tried to hide myself, to not give myself away. I wanted to show that I was good, that I was kind, that I followed the rules. My brothers could break them, had the freedom in themselves to not care about disapproval, but I had a secret to keep, and guarded it by shoring up my personality against any repri-mand. It was a sort of displacement of shame. While I boxed off the part of myself I knew I couldn't let show, I magni-fied others, over-identifying with anything I might use as protection. Education, religion, middle-class privilege, any-thing I could get hold of. They were my suit of armour, the uniform of my cohesion. That early sense of shame went underground: in protecting myself, in choosing which parts of myself to hide and which to magnify, I fragmented myself. I made a hierarchy of each facet of my identity, and at the bottom of the shaky, unstable tower I called 'myself' there was a little locked box.

I was brought up vaguely Catholic, mainly as a way not to disappoint my grandmother, but on occasional Sundays we went to church. When I sat in the pew and saw the priest at the pulpit and heard the parables and sermons, all those tales of goodness, I knew that was my road to acceptance. If I could blend in here, I was safe. I felt that I was being offered a key to life. Unlike my brothers, I made my visits to church dutifully, and went to Sunday school. The old women loved me, fussed over me, pulled my cheeks until they hurt, and I paraded myself for them. Every warm smile was an acceptance, a sign of my passing undetected. Per-haps, even then, I was in the habit of atoning for myself.

Perhaps, even then, I was a little Hopkins, marking out my sins, hiding them away, looking for love.

In my late teens I went each year to volunteer with the pilgrimage at Lourdes. It was an eery, eerily perfect place. The baths in the Sanctuary there were cut into the hillside behind the crypt and, above them, a brutalist concrete roof extended over the rows of metal barricades where the people queued, some pushing wheelchairs, others solemnly telling their beads, all waiting in line to be washed, to be blessed, to be cured. Alongside the building, an opalescent river, the water an unearthly green, tumbled in icy sprays and barrels of current. Set against the clean grey and gold of the basilica, and the steep, snow-capped mountains in the distance, the whole domain was unsettlingly, almost self-righteously, pristine.

This is where, as we were often reminded, the fifteen-year-old Bernadette Soubirous saw, over a series of months, the apparition of a young lady, standing inside a cave. I pictured it often: a windless day, a reef of sun-topped clouds unmoving in the calm blue of the sky, and Bernadette sitting alone, watching the wavelets of the Savy slide into the Gave, the larger river's muscles kneading and twisting as it carried itself downstream. I can still travel back to that vision, so strong a hold it took in my teenage mind. In it, Bernadette is contemplating crossing the river, but as she takes off her wooden shoes and puts her feet into the water, she notices a change in the light – something leaden, overcast – and then, looking forward into the cavern ahead, into the deepest part of it, she sees a sort of radiance, as though all the golden light of the evening has been caught there in the cleft of the rock. And then, staring harder, mesmerised, she sees, standing in the grotto, a woman. Short, wearing white clothes cut neatly about her delicate waist, and barefoot. Her tiny, narrow feet are unblemished, almost alabaster.

I could imagine the held breath, the moment of utter awe. Every time I passed the grotto, I thought of that. Just the river-water playing its fluorescence over the roof of the cave, the weird shifting of the atmosphere, and these two women staring at each other, one in dumb amazement or fright, the other calmly, full of reassurance. Doubted in her day, the Virgin knew what faith was, and she knew what the world thought of women who have it. Everywhere in Lourdes I was reminded of that miracle – the faith of the teenager, her persistence, the doubt of the world against which she held a quiet, tenacious opposition. Also, the linking of women: the matrilineal looping of time as one hand reaches out across the centuries to hold the other.

Since her burial, Bernadette's body, we were told, had not decomposed, though it had been exhumed three times, partly to provide evidence of its miraculous state, and partly to allow relics (in this case, two of her right ribs) to be removed and sent to Rome. Covered in wax, she slept now inside a crystal reliquary, her head on a plump white pillow. Visitors to the convent of Saint Gildard could see her laid out in a glass casket behind an altar rail, bathed in the blue light of six stained-glass windows. I heard whispers from other pilgrims who said it was true, they'd been there, they'd seen it.

When Mary appeared to Bernadette, she told her about a spring, which rose from the grotto and runs now into a great reservoir built below the basilica. A whole complex has been erected around it. The water is pumped up through a number of fountains, where pilgrims fill small plastic bottles in the shape of the Virgin, or collect it into big containers to be taken home. As I stood there, on my first visit, the roof of the cave was damp, beaded and dripping, and was sewing the smooth puddles on the floor with perfect seeds of water. One of my friends, a member of my parish group, filled six twenty-litre containers. Later, we drove them home in the back of our minibus, through France, across the Channel, and over most of the length of England, so that her mother, diagnosed with cancer, could bathe in it.

Not far from the cave were the baths, where the water was pumped up from the source into a series of grey marble tubs. It was here, one afternoon, that I joined the other pilgrims and stood in line. The old man whose care I had been assigned for the day had asked me, after lighting his votary and muttering an insistent prayer for his dead wife, to take him down to the baths in the hope that the arthritis in his hip might be eased by the healing water. Out of curiosity, mainly, but also some solemn sense of purpose, I thought that I, too, might go inside.

There were two entrances. Both were covered with striped blue-and-white curtains and ringed with a garland of white silk roses. I watched as, one by one, the people were called forward and walked nervously through the curtain and into the room beyond. I could hear the water splashing inside and the constant recitation of the rosary lifting like a drone through the building. Not knowing what was behind the curtain, I was apprehensive, my knees shuddering with the nerves. My schoolboy French was enough to get by, but it couldn't hope to cover the occult intricacies of ritual and prayer I imagined to take place in the veiled world of the baths. Likewise, though I had attended church often enough, and taken the tests for confirmation, there was a devout, European intensity to the Catholicism of

Lourdes that the English strain of my home town never came close to, and I was afraid of being asked for some unknown prayer, or required to perform a sort of genuflection with which I was unfamiliar. Added to this was the acute teenage fear of nudity, of being seen in my body by a room of strangers.

Once I was ushered through the first curtain, the world took on a sense of unreality. Echoing voices caught in water, high-pitched drops of water falling from the stones. In the background, a chant of prayer was punctuated occasionally by the crash of cold waters as a body was submerged and then lifted. Inside this first room, two men came and stood on either side of me. They held up a blue sheet, so that I could undress between them, and then they wrapped me tightly in it and asked me to sit down again. I had never been naked among strangers before. Swaddled and uncomfortable on the wooden slats of the benches, I tried awkwardly not to look at the other men. Most of them were old; ill, I thought, in some indefinable way I could not diagnose by the movements of their frail torsos. Watching them, I felt an unnerving sensation, an anxiety, as though I, too, were one of the dying; waiting here, goosebumps sharpening along my arms, my nipples tight and cold, hoping somehow to fix whatever it was that was wrong with me. Perhaps each of them looked at me in turn – the pale young man, sitting awkwardly in his blue sheet – and pitied me. Perhaps they imagined some cruel virus multiplying inside me as I made a last-ditch appeal to faith, my prayer to a god who might, at this late hour, show his face.

One by one, we were beckoned through a second curtain, each of us standing when called and walking solemnly, nervously, through to the other side. When my turn came, I went between the wet slats of the curtain and into the chamber beyond. The room was split on two levels – the lower level was set with a deep marble bath, the clear water rocking inside, and above it (at eye level with me as I stood on the raised floor) was a small white statuette of the Virgin, who was looking down peacefully over the scene below, her miniature hands lifted together in prayer. All the walls were tiled in a grey slate which glistened and sweated, seeming to replicate the grotto at the riverside.

There were two other men in the room. After I entered, they took off my blue sheet and wrapped me quickly in a white cotton one, damp and translucent, and bound me in it tightly, so that my penis was pressed uncomfortably upwards. There was no time to adjust myself, no time when I wasn't being watched. The two men led me down the three stone steps into the bath and told me, in French, to look up at the Virgin. I did so, obediently focusing on her. A prayer was said and I ended with an uncertain 'Amen', a sign of the cross, before the men put their hands on to me – one on my chest, one on my back – and sank me down into the water, which shattered beneath me with a loud crash, and then remade itself across me.

When I came back up, I gasped for a few seconds, and then wiped my palms over my eyes and opened them again. Above me, I noticed the delicate play of the shadows on the ceiling, the light refracting and regathering its forms, and thought of Bernadette. There was something about the way the light broke in the water, how it rippled and projected its image upwards, that seemed mesmeric. Everything was sound and light, and I was standing inside it. The lucent, liquid webbing of the light made shapes that mounted one another and then gave way, the rays finding themselves in the prism of the water and being made visible over the ceiling, being unclothed and reclothed, slipping from one dimension into another. After their official prayer, I said a small prayer of my own, not really to God, but to myself.

Most of us who got that minibus from the north-west of England to the south-west of France each year were non-believers. I remember one of the group, an older girl, saying that the more you came to Lourdes, the less you believed. I had a secret faith, but compared with the relative coolness of the congregation in England, the devotion and fervour of this gathering was alien. Here, people would speak with absolute conviction about faith healing and purgatory, about apparitions and relics. They cried openly like children when they ran their hands along the bare rock of the grotto; they walked in procession with bowed heads and sang hymns without any of the irony or smirks we used to exchange throughout Mass at home. There was something wild about the displays of devotion, and something xenophobic, I'm sure, in our distaste for it. Groups of men would carry huge candles over their shoulders and walk them down to the votive stalls. 'The bigger the candle . . .' I joked, nudging my friend with my elbow as the men walked by.

You could buy reams of rosaries and statuettes. One stall even offered dinner plates painted with an image of the grotto and the Virgin, on to which families could have their photograph transposed. Each year we would hunt for the tackiest souvenirs. Once, I found a life-size cut-out of Christ, which was overlain with a hologram. As you walked past, the smiling, peaceful face of the saviour would gradually turn into a bloodied look of pain, and a crown of thorns appeared, cutting down into the skin of his forehead. My friend found a cigarette lighter decorated with an image of the Holy Family. Another girl skipped joyously towards us, holding out a pen. It was like ones we had found in seafront shops in Blackpool, where if you held it upright, the woman's clothes would slide off. But here, when the pen was tipped, a tiny Virgin Mary would descend into the grotto scene inlaid on the side.

In many ways, though, Lourdes seemed a desperate place, and perhaps our youthful aversion was to that, too. The dying and the sick and the devout hurled themselves here yearly into a defiant flourishing that seemed, as we watched them, immensely sad. Rather than a strength of faith, we came to see a group of people caught in the final throws of belief, reaching out over and over to feel themselves loved, to imagine that some great power might save them from the lives they had the misfortune of living. But it was also a place of unmatched calm. At night, after the candlelit processions had wound through the arches of the basilica, the nuns would walk in pairs back to the hospital or to their accommodation, chattering like schoolgirls. They would smile benevolently at us when we passed. Great stalls of votive candles were lit, and the thousand little flames flickered in the evening and in the blue water of the river.

Then, after we had taken the sick people back to the hospitals after the final Mass, the city turned again, revealing a new face. We would stroll down in our groups, sunburnt and tired, to one of the bars by the river – the Carrefour or the Jeanne d'Arc – and buy pints of Kronenbourg until the day spiralled away into a great confusion of drinking. As with all gatherings of teenagers, the banks of the Gave de Pau after sunset became a place of tentative sexual exploration: emissaries were sent from one parish group to another; handsome boys were gossiped about with increasing fervour as the nights passed by. Each year, there was a new boy I fell in love with, a new boy I knew I could never tell. I longed for the freedom of the others. I would have given anything to drunkenly kiss a stranger by the river, to imagine a future with them, to have it dashed.

And yet, alongside all of this existed the familiar world of the Church. In order to share a hotel room with my (female) friend I had to pretend for the whole trip that I was her cousin. She knew I was gay and it was a sort of in-joke we had. If we got into trouble with the nuns, I would say, 'My cousin's a bit hungover this morning,' smirking, trying not to laugh. Although I doubt the volunteers from the other parishes would have cared too much about my sexuality, it was a tacit understanding between the group that we kept it shrouded from the adults and the nuns and the nurses and the sick people we spent our days caring for. A thousand little lies, all neatly stitched into a protective barrier, though I wasn't sure if it was myself or the religious that I was protecting. It was as though we lived in two temporalities, shifting between them. Perhaps that is what teenagers do best. There were the older generations and the Church on the one hand, and on the other the irreverent, secret life of the young.

Once, a group of us got so drunk that we wandered down into the domain, exploring. We weren't supposed to be there after dark, but that silent, sacred space beyond the river was too tempting – it sang to us, calling us towards it. We walked by the rows of pollarded trees, their fists of leaf held to the sky, and then stopped at the foot of the fountain on the main plaza, the Virgin looking down on us from between the shooting ropes of water. Three nuns walked past through the archways, arm in arm, and we turned away, stifling laughter, hiding in the shadows. I was distracted by the emptiness, the statues and the basilica veiled in the blue haze of the summer evening, and when I turned around to catch up with the others I noticed that my friend – the one I shared a room with all week, my 'cousin' – was talking in hushed urgency with another girl, just a little further along the main approach. I saw them draw closer, hugging each other, and then watched the familiar juddering of their shoulders as they started to cry. An inconsolable heft of sadness was working its rhythm through them. I didn't know whether to go over, whether to offer some comfort, or to leave them alone. The beer was swaying me, too, and I assumed it was nothing, just too much drink; so I wandered off over to the votive stalls by the river, where a cool breeze was lifting and the thousand little flames made a mirage against the tree-shadows and the purpled glow of the moon.

As I stood in front of the rows of candles, all these bright petals of fire flickering and moving in the gentle sway of wind from the river, a stillness seemed to expand around me. I was transfixed. The candles moved and danced, innumerable small offerings of hope. Each life I had known, and each life I hadn't, glimmered in front of me, and I thought of all the people, everyone who had lived and everyone who hadn't. All the bright energy of the world was being lifted through each wick and set aflame, and I felt it rising in me, too. I can't remember when I started to cry, but once I did, a grief I hadn't known possible was drawn through me, a flood of it rising and pulsing outwards, and I couldn't stop it and I didn't want to. I think I was crying for myself, too – the world I was leaving behind, the safety of it, the sealed, hypocritical life I was living and couldn't live any more. I was saying goodbye to the self I had prayed for, to this ruinous safety I had made for myself to inhabit. The worst part of all was that I didn't know where I would go next, and I couldn't be sure who out of my family or my friends would follow me there.

*

For too long I had chosen to cohabit with the world's tacit disdain. Then, before I realised what was happening, the people I had hidden behind turned against me. It was as though I had been walking step by step with an advancing army, and then suddenly there were whispers, movements, and one by one the faces turned and looked at me, the stranger in their ranks. When I was twenty and the issue of equal marriage rights was raised in Parliament, something old and almost archaic woke up.

As the draft bill moved through Parliament, the opposition was often fierce and brutal. The Catholic Church wrote to every state-funded Catholic school in the country, asking them to encourage pupils to sign a petition against the proposal. Politicians compared equal marriage rights to bestiality; a cardinal likened it to the legalisation of slavery. For the whole time I was alive, this machine had been turning on people, but now it had turned on me. All of a sudden, it was me who was discussed in public, on the news, in the houses of friends and relatives over dinner, in the houses of Parliament over the jeers of full benches. The old institutions I had hidden behind seemed to blaze in a final fury. The pulpits of Britain, in some unlikely twist, became once more a place of explicit politics. The smiling priests of my youth, the ones I had shared walks with in Lourdes, who had blessed me at Mass, stood up and denounced me. In the end, after the process of a few years, the bill passed with a majority, but it didn't feel like a confirmation of anything. The shock of being debated, of being fought both for and against, of being subjected to constant conversation, made me feel exposed and degraded.

As I listened, I felt a deep schism opening between myself and the people and institutions I had loved. But as the rift widened over time, I began to feel more free. The ties between myself and my world, the ones that had held me down, were being cut. My body and my queerness and my life became inseparable. Through that splitting away, I felt myself becoming irrevocably and radically whole.

When our parish priest stood up in church one Sunday and read out the official statement from the archbishops, which was circulated to every parish in the country to solidify opposition to the vote, my mother stood up and left. I imagined the sound of the church door slamming behind her, echoing through the building. In my university bedroom I read the statement online. 'The roots of the institution of marriage lie in our nature,' the archbishops wrote, neatly informing their congregants who was natural and who was not. Marriage, it said, was 'an expression of our fundamental humanity'. The pronoun 'our' did not include me. I am ashamed to say that I only understood the depth of my own collusion in this way of thinking when I saw it turn so starkly against me. Everything contrary to it was 'disordered', 'unnatural', outside the bounds of grace. I was sure, then, that if anything was intrinsically disordered, it was the Catholic Church. If anything was contrary to nature it was harnessing an idea of nature and weaponising it. It wasn't my nature; it wasn't the nature Hopkins had shown me. At my desk, I composed a letter to the diocese, declaring (rather grandiosely) my defection from the Church. I was sickened by the idea that my name could be counted amongst the legion of believers who might be enlisted as a bargaining chip against the legislation. After a month or so I received a letter to tell me that the process for defecting had been closed. Convenient timing, no doubt.

Integration, I realised, had split me. Now, finally detached, I felt alive, I felt free. I had looked into the mirror of my country and had seen my own irreconcilable difference. The world I had defended – and into which I had intertwined myself – did not love me. I knew that now. Still, they had something I wanted: they had stolen my God from me. That idea of God, of a world that, if touched rightly, might 'give off sparks and take fire, yield drops and flow, ring and tell of him', was something I couldn't let go of. I would steal my God back. I would run with him through the burning streets.

I never returned to church, but I found that it wasn't so easy to separate myself. I had become myself while wearing that armour – the shape of myself was moulded by it, the routines of my body coloured by its sounds and movement, the imagery of my mind rinsed with it. The Church, and all those other accoutrements, ran through me like water flowing through a sediment. I brought Hopkins with me out of the wreckage. I brought a changed image of God with me. When I swam and lifted myself out on to the shore, I felt the light of rebirth. When I saw the million forms of the earth playing in the sun, I thought of my old God, disembodied, and set free.

*

One night, after all this, the year after Elias and I broke up, I was awake late, back in Liverpool, wandering in the park behind my house, taking my usual route along the side of the lake. I was haunted by what had happened over those years. I had looked too long into the darkness and the darkness had looked back. My nerves were pricked and on edge. There was hardly any moon and everything was reduced to silhouette and to sound. As I passed the rushes by the curve of the lake, a sleeping coot woke suddenly and unloosed its high, round cry. It startled me and I found myself fearing that there was another figure approaching behind me on the path.

By the far side of the water, the horse chestnut was already blooming, its pink cones of flower held up, still lit somehow in the night. I watched the dark form of the tree standing in silence, and up in the branches some darker shape – oval and somewhat leaning – was lodged there, cloaked and unsettlingly defined against all the obscurity of the clouds and the soft threshing of the leaves. Perhaps I was being watched after all. I walked closer, nervously, taking each step carefully over the slick path in case I spooked whatever was up there; forming some strange fantasy that it might swoop down, talons opened on to the tender skin of my scalp. In any other year I might have been curious, but now I imagined myself clashing and swiping my hands over my head wildly, trying to knock whatever sharp-beaked thing came hurtling out of the air with a thud of my fist. I no longer trusted the world.

When I got under the shadow of the tree, I looked up, craning my neck upwards as far as I could. I stood for some time trying to figure out the shape of the thing. It was like a black hole in the night, a suffusion of darkness that felt both real and metaphorical. Then, it moved: it was a heron, head crooked downwards, asleep high above the pond. And for some reason, in that instant, the aperture of my mind closed. I panicked and ran. It was hard to know, then, where fear ended and reality began, and here in the shape of the bird I could hardly separate the forms of my mind from the forms of the world. I wasn't inventing my fear: the world itself was haunted and sinister, was waiting in the branches at night for me to walk unsuspectingly by. I ran, not looking back, along the side of the lake, through the garden gate, up the wooden steps and into the flat, closing the door behind me and locking it.

Back home, in my room, I felt vulnerable and alone. The orange glow of the street lamps outside my window spread over the ceiling, and the shadows of people walking along the pavement elongated over the white plaster. As the people passed, the black forms shrunk and clustered across the cornicing until they vanished and were gone. I lay under the covers, freezing, the draught of a breeze cluttering the shutters occasionally, and my nose wet with the cold. My bed leant against a boarded-up chimney breast, and inside I could hear voices echoing from the flats above, carrying through the hollow passages of the building. Laughing, then silence; then, again, a voice.

I did what I always did that year, when I was alone and heartsore: took out my phone and tried to find someone to prise the light back in. Scrolling through the bright screen of photographs, messages buzzing through, I felt connected and desired. Eventually, I found a man who wanted to come over. He was short, older than me, with dark hair and bright grey eyes and an odd innocence I couldn't place. When I opened the door of the building he barely met my gaze, just ducked past me and hurried into the flat. He was furtive, like a man on the run, a man being watched. I closed the heavy blue door and clicked the latch, pointed him to the door of my room, which was ajar, and watched as he went inside. I had barely seen his face. When I followed him into the room, he was standing by the bed and walked across to me. He hardly spoke. When I leant my face to his, at first he was quiet, then urgent, utilitarian. There was a sense of frustration and necessity to his movements, his hurried undressing, the lack of even friendly conversation or the forced banter I was used to.

Straight afterwards he got up to wash, standing over the sink in the bathroom and splashing water over his face and neck and hands like a bird shivering itself clean. I could see him through the frosted glass of the bathroom door, which swung open on its hinge behind him. After he was done, he looked up at me, meeting my gaze. In a hushed voice, quite serious, he told me that he was in training for the priesthood. The priest who carried out home visits here, who I spoke to sometimes in the building's communal garden, was his mentor. The priest's car, an old duck-egg Fiat, was parked near the entrance. The man needed to be invisible, to get out without being seen. I nodded my understanding, and scanned the hallway before I gave him the signal that no one was outside. By the door, he checked his pockets ('Keys? Wallet? Presbytery keys?') then left. Had he really just said that? I stood there, quietly stunned, as the latch clicked back into place. It was as though I had met a different version of myself. I felt sad, then comforted. There, walking off into the night, turning the key in his car and driving away, was a man I had escaped from being. But there was also a man who had not escaped.

*

I looked up at Elias as we sat on one of the white metal tables outside the hospital, in some rare autumn sunlight – blue sky, the leaves of an arching sycamore bright yellow, and no wind to strew them over the car park or along the long street down the hill. Earlier that day he had a meeting, just himself and a nurse and the consultant. They had told him that they thought he might be ready to leave the ward, and he told me that he hadn't made any reply. Instead, he'd looked at them, like he was a child and they were his parents, and he realised then that he couldn't leave, that he wasn't ready to go. This wasn't, he assured me, because he thought he might try to kill himself, though he made no promises there, either. He was scared.

'Jag är så rädd,' he said, to himself, shaking his head. I'm so scared. *'Jag kan inte. Jag kan inte. Jag kan inte.'* I can't. I can't. I can't.

He worked himself up, just saying it, stressing the *kan* over and over again, reinforcing the impossibility of it all. How could he go back home? How could he see his friends? How could he ever show his face in the world again?

In taking away all his power, all his capacity for making decisions, the past month at the hospital had also done something to take away his anxiety, to stall time, to set in abeyance all those unanswerable, unfathomable possibilities that lay ahead once the clock was wound again, and set ticking.

'Du kan, Elias,' I whispered, to him but also to myself, willing myself to believe it. *'Du måste.'* You must.

There was no map for the world in which we had found ourselves. I would have said to him, 'There is only one way forward,' but I knew now that there were two ways, and that other dark future hung over the conversation, hung over all of our conversations, a constant threat, a constant perched watcher, ready to swoop. I squeezed his hand. My fingers pressed around his knuckles so hard that he pulled away and said, '*Oj!*' and laughed, almost a real laugh, and the sun broke again through the branches of the sycamore, and for a moment it loosed a pattern of light over him, all across his legs and his bare arms, and he closed his eyes and leant back into its brief warmth, the leaf-patterns playing over his face as he exhaled, until the tree settled again, and the shadow of it reassembled itself across him.

V

There were times when I thought Elias would never leave the hospital. The longer he stayed in there, the more insurmountable the idea of leaving became. For me, the outside world was a place full of sinister possibilities, sinister intent. For him, it was a place where time drudged forward, relentlessly, where life carried on. The limbo of the ward was numbing and safe. Lifted outside of the world, it allowed us to hold life in abeyance. Time, like a river, flowed quietly past us, never bearing us with it.

When Elias was sitting in his bedroom, a few days before he was finally signed out, I left his room and walked the corridor without telling him. I was looking for the consultant.

'I don't think it's safe for him to leave,' I blurted out, as she closed the office door.

She turned and looked at me, kindly, searching my face, trying to read me.

'Has he said anything to make you . . . ?' She paused to find the word. 'Concerned?'

Many things, I thought. And there were things he hadn't said, too. I could see it in his eyes sometimes, that desperation, that exhaustion. I told her what he had told me, about still wanting to die, and she nodded, calmly. Of course – she had spoken to him, too.

'The thing is, this isn't a prison. If he wants to leave, we can't lock him inside.'

I exhaled, frustrated, still frightened. 'Can't you?'

I couldn't trust why Elias wanted to go. I knew the hospital was threatening his sense of self, his independence, but it was also secure. Selfishly, I wanted the reassurance that he was safe. I was scared of having the whole responsibility of his life placed into my keeping. As much as I wanted to believe him, to meet his need to be trusted, I worried that he was planning something, another escape, and this time, I thought, this time I might not be there to stop him. I could feel myself being overbearing, controlling, but I couldn't dislodge the thought that it was all a collusion, a trick, that I was falling for it all over again. Once the doctors were gone, and the nurses, and the other patients, there would just be me and Elias.

We had signed the lease for an unfurnished studio flat the week before his birthday, before everything happened, and had never moved into it. On the day we left the hospital – a month after Elias was admitted – his father drove us into town on his way to work and dropped us off at our new apartment building. It was Elias who had chosen the place, who had met with the letting agents. He had been so capable, so self-sufficient. It seemed like another life altogether.

The building was a three-storey, pre-war block, and was at the top of a steep road on a hill to the edge of the city centre, set high enough to see out across the roads and the houses on a clear day to the docks and the sea beyond. There were woods around it – silver birches and oaks, mainly, all stripped bare now by wind – but the road down to the city was steep enough that from the front of the building you could peer out over the tops of the trees, their branches waving and scratching underneath the sky. Elias's father pulled over into the small parking bay outside, leaving his indicator ticking as we got out with our suitcases and two sports bags stuffed with bedding, and then he drove off to work, waving into the rear-view mirror as the car turned the corner. Just the two of us now.

Elias took out the set of keys at the main door and we walked up the stone spiral steps to our apartment, taking the bags up with us, and went inside. The apartment was painted a faint green, not dissimilar to the green of the hospital ward. It was fitted with old, square parquet flooring that echoed as the door closed behind us. The wood squeaked under our wet shoes as we dragged the luggage across it. Elias looked hollow, his eyes dark.

The echo of the room seemed to confirm our aloneness. We slid off our shoes and kicked them to the side of the small hallway, hung our coats and scarves up on the door hooks, and pulled the damp, woollen gloves off our hands. I eyed those door hooks for a second, and then the light fixtures, the curtain rail. Just the two of us, I thought. The studio had one main room, with a small kitchen off to one side, and it had seemed big enough when it was empty, but I knew it wouldn't take much before it became cramped. I had ordered a bed, which had been delivered while we were away and signed for by Elias's father, and it turned out now that the thing was so big it took up nearly a third of the main room, so there was just enough space left for us to put a sofa and a small table. Elias showed me around, vaguely recalling what the letting agent had told him. He followed her routine: opening the cupboards in the kitchen, pointing out the heating panel and where the light switches were. I flicked them on and off, and nodded, as if I were testing the dashboard of an unfamiliar car.

In the ward everything had been taken care of. Independence was traded in for safety. Whereas the hospital was regimented, contained, life outside was unpredictable. I didn't know if I would be able to leave the apartment without Elias. I didn't know if I could sleep, not knowing if he was sleeping, too, or if he had snuck out again. I couldn't protect both of us at the same time. Besides, I didn't really know what protection looked like, or what healing looked like, or how it was done. There were no scans, no X-rays, no medicine that would fix things completely.

We sat at the end of the bed, and I lay back on it. I said something about how comfortable it was, wanting to reassure Elias that everything was going to be OK, to sell this new world to him all over again. I wanted him to know that he'd chosen a good apartment, that life here was possible. I went into the hall and opened one of the sports bags, taking out the bedding, and threw the duvet and pillows across the bed, which seemed to at least gesture towards the idea that this was our apartment and that we would be living here. When I finished, he didn't move. He was just staring, not quite *out* of the window, but *at* it, as though everything beyond it – the bare silver birches, the scrubbed grass, the pathway to the road – were unreal, a daydream he wasn't a part of.

'Should we get some food?'

He jerked his head, surprised by my voice, and then looked around, as though he wasn't sure he knew what it meant to *want* anything at all.

'There's a takeaway at the top of the hill. I can call them.'

I knew he was scared about seeing people. Seeing people meant having to act in a certain way. He was scared about them asking questions, about them knowing where he had

been and what had happened. I picked up the phone and
called them. The woman on the other end of the line
explained that they didn't deliver; it was collection only. I
felt a sudden dip in my gut, a deep anxiety about going out
and leaving Elias alone. Still, I wanted to try my best to trust
him, to show him that I trusted him, to give him even this
small independence.

'*Jag förstår*,' I said to the woman on the phone. '*Jag kommer snart.*' My broken Swedish was just enough to brave
these small interactions.

I picked up my wallet and went to put my shoes back on,
looking around the apartment, checking it by instinct. The
plug sockets, the oven, the drawer of knives. Elias looked
up at me.

'What?'

'Nothing,' I said. 'It doesn't matter. I'll be back soon.'

As I closed the heavy door behind me and stepped outside, the wind whirled and stung my face. It was bitterly
cold. I hurried up the path around the building and looked
back into the window of our flat. I was standing now in the
view directly outside, as though I were a figure in that daydream world.

I couldn't see Elias. Was he lying down? Was he in the
hallway? I shook myself and turned around. It was OK, I
could trust him. I'd only be gone for ten minutes.

Still, as soon as I got to the takeaway, I took out my
phone. Before I knew what I was doing, I was calling his
number. My heart slowed to a dull thud as the rings repeated.

No answer. Fuck. No answer. Five rings. Ten rings. Then,
a click: he picked up. I stuttered, not knowing what to say.

'Erm . . . Erm . . . Do you . . . ? Do you want a drink?'

He answered yes, unenthusiastically.

'OK. I'll be back soon.'

In the space of those rings, my heart seemed to have vanished – I could barely feel it inside myself.

A quarter of an hour later, after the confusion of trying to order sushi in Swedish, I came back with a tray of salmon rolls, two cartons of miso soup, and a couple of bottles of Mariestads lager. When I opened the door, Elias was standing in the hallway, putting the empty sports bags on to a high shelf, as though he had been unpacking. He ate standing at the counter, and I sat cross-legged on the floor, leaning against the kitchen wall.

In the early afternoon his mother came over with a paper bag of cinnamon buns and Tupperware packed with food for the freezer, looking nervous, and doing the rounds of the small apartment as I had done, full of praise for it, saying how cosy it would be once we'd settled in, how nice the building was, how good it was to be up on the hill with the woods around us and the shops so close by. She looked over at Elias occasionally, checking as I had done to see whether the praise was registering, anxious about how he was feeling. I made some tea, boiling the water in a pan on the stove, and we stood around with the cups steaming in our faces.

'We could go to the shops to look for some furniture?' she said, her rising intonation already suggesting that she expected to be cut down.

Elias looked up at me, his eyes imploring me to help. Any small disturbances had the potential to send his fragile stability shattering.

'Don't worry,' she said, taking his hand. 'We'll go out of town. And it's a Wednesday, anyway. It'll be quiet. There won't be anyone there.'

I looked into Elias's wide eyes and smiled, nodding. '*Ska vi*?'

Quietly, Elias agreed.

In the blue Volvo I was already steeling myself, anticipating something, trying to think ahead. What if we met one of his friends? What if he ran away? We turned out of the apartment, down the narrow hill-road and out on to the carriageway. Ten minutes later we got caught in the traffic lights waiting for the trams to leave at Korsvägen. I closed my eyes and remembered that other time when I had been driven through that junction, desperately willing the lights to change, with Elias out at the summerhouse, his faltering voice on the phone. I opened my eyes and looked into the rearview mirror. He was in the backseat now, leaning his forehead against the cold window. The grey light played across his empty face, the clean glass shimmering it over his body.

As we drove out on to the roundabout, the pull of force as the car turned hauled his body upright. He was tired, passive, carried along by the world. We drove out along the motorway north for a few junctions, then turned off on to a narrower road through the woods. Now, some of the pines had turned bright yellow, their golden, shaggy needles still held to the branches. They looked like apostles in a fresco. On the radio the presenter read through the headlines of the local news – a new shopping centre was being built; a school was having a fête; a man was interviewed about the effects of some EU legislation I couldn't quite get the sense of. As usual, the signal began to falter, the voices distorting. Elias's mother turned it down and all we could hear then was the drumming of the road beneath us. Some of the pine-scent, still damp from the night before, drifted in through the closed windows.

It was always like this in the forests: the quietness, the perceptible downshift in the gears. The road snaked through the tall pines, which rose so high above it I could only make out a road-width of sky through the sunroof. It was like driving through a gorge, and beside us the trees crowded so thickly that, if I looked into the forest for too long, the rush of the trunks passing by made me queasy. It was impossible to focus. Everything was thrown into a whirl of colour and movement. Occasionally, a silver flash of sun would appear through a gap in the woods – a lake or a peat-pool acting like a mirror – and then the pines would hurry back, swallowing it into a thicket of deep, oppressive green.

The Swedes knew to drive cautiously when the woods were deep. They had warned me about them, and so I knew exactly what happened when an elk or a stag burst running into the road and there was no time to stop the car. Crumpled metal, smashed skulls, the steaming body split open on the tarmac. I found I was bracing myself for the hurtling body, the sudden, sickening crash, but it never came. After a few miles of hushed driving, we turned off the road at the edge of the forest and found the place we were looking for. It was less like a thrift shop than a warehouse, tucked away in a lorry park, but the outside was ringed with fairy lights, and staff were helping people to load furniture into their cars, or were packing it off into vans for delivery. There was a café by the entrance door, where a few couples were sitting, their shopping bags tucked beneath the tables. We got out of the car and Elias kept his head down as though he were exposed, as though everyone would turn in hushed silence and watch him walk across the car park, knowing what he had done. He wore his hood up over his face, shielding himself, like a child making himself invisible.

Inside, the warehouse was huge. High-ceilinged, strip-lit, stacked with furniture, clothes, books, kitchen appliances, and shelves and shelves of cheap antiques. We had a list of things we needed: lamps, a coffee table, a sofa. As we walked through the aisles, Elias seemed to gradually relax – the place had only a few people, mostly elderly women, and the activity of looking for furniture seemed to give him a way to think outside himself, to consider our room at home and its possible contents, rather than his mind's endless lancing questions.

Near the entrance I was distracted by the second-hand coats, admiring the sheer weight of them, all that heft to keep out the cold of a Swedish winter. At first, Elias and his mother looked through them, too, but at some point they must have wandered off. I found an old Gant coat – knee-length, navy, with a brown leather collar. It was too big even for me, but I loved how it fastened up high around the throat and had low, deep pockets. I put it on and kept the hanger in my hand, turning around with a smile on my face, knowing both of them would tell me it was too big, too old, too tattered, but neither of them was there.

I craned my head over the rails, but I couldn't see them. Through the bric-a-brac, the children's clothes, and the toys – no sign. By the time I had caught up, Elias's mother was already sitting on a low, burgundy couch, stroking the fabric, and Elias was bending over, looking at the short wooden legs as though he were inspecting them, checking to see if they were chipped or scratched. I stopped before they saw me, and stood back amongst the clothing rails, watching. His mother was talking and Elias was down on his knees at one corner of the couch. He got up and walked to the next corner, where he bent again to look at the wooden leg. My heart fluttered uncomfortably. What I saw, watching him, was a small hope, a fragile thing more precious because it thought itself unobserved. My old self seemed to lift to the surface. I felt it. It was as though my body was reinhabited after so long standing empty. There was something of the old Elias, too – intent and thorough, detailed, practical. Checking the legs of the sofa, one by one, and examining the fabric for patches of wear, I saw him looking to see if the furniture would last, wondering whether it was worth the money, whether it would go well in the apartment, whether he wanted it to be his sofa or not. Time, for a brief moment, collapsed, and the past and present linked over the preceding month, flowing around it. There he was: the old Elias, considering, tentatively, a small investment in the future.

As I stood amongst the clothing rails and watched, one hand in the pocket of my big coat, the other still holding the hanger, Elias sat down next to his mother on the sofa and leant against the padded arm. When I walked over, I wanted to be casual. I was nervous, then and later, about looking something so everyday in the eye, as though the old Elias might startle and retreat under my gaze.

I went over to the front of the sofa and shrugged my coat.

'What do you think?'

Elias looked up at me – my Elias, as though he had never left.

'I think you should buy it,' he said, and as he reached out to touch the fabric of the coat, he squeezed my arm gently.

'Me too,' I whispered, smiling at my own luck. 'And the couch, are you taking it? It's lovely.'

He nodded, patting it, as if to prove it was sturdy. An

assistant came over and wrote Elias's name down on a pad of copy paper, then tore off the first page, stuck it to the couch, and gave us the fainter yellow slip from underneath where the name was just about visible in the tracing.

Buoyed, we set off in search of lamps, a coffee table, some pots and pans for the kitchen. I found a room at the back of the warehouse, sectioned off with partitions, full of records and old books. I flicked through the old LPs, then ran my eyes over the bookcases. Here there were thousands and thousands of stories, textbooks, crime thrillers and classics, all well-thumbed, some of them foxed and split along the spine. There was a table, too, of plays and poetry books, and I picked up a few, leafing through them, considering them, putting them back. At the end of the table was a stack of small, fabric-covered hardbacks. None of them had dust jackets – just names embossed along the spines, names I didn't know: Pär Lagerkvist, Edith Södergran, Harry Martinson, Karin Boye. I wanted to remember that day, to have a souvenir of its tiny hopeful hour. Then I heard Elias behind me.

'I knew you'd be here.'

I picked up the four books, showing them to him, and he nodded at the names, picking out the blue book and letting it fall open in his palm.

'I like her,' he said. 'Karin Boye. She was from Gothenburg, too.'

*

The furniture was delivered the same day – the van almost beating us home – and after we'd carried it all up the stairs and into the apartment, we were aching and tired. Still, it felt as though a seal had been broken: if only for a few hours, we'd been outside, around people, and nothing had gone wrong. Perhaps, I thought, things would get easier now that Elias had seen he could do it.

After only a few hours, though, Elias sunk back into himself. He went quiet and glazed. He was exhausted with speaking, with the day's exposure, and I worried that we'd pushed him too far, had done too much too soon. He lay on the bed and I lay on the new burgundy sofa, under the glow of the marble-based standing lamp we'd bought, and I picked up the four cloth-bound books of poetry, which were stacked on the coffee table. I looked again at the names on the spines: Pär Lagerkvist, Edith Södergran, Harry Martinson, Karin Boye. Each book was from the same edition, some series of modernist poets.

I took up the Lagerkvist first, an amber-yellow book, and leafed through it. The room was quiet, the wind occasionally gusting through the bare trees outside and flashing patterns through the window, and I felt guilty. All my well-meant attempts to draw Elias out, to bring him back into the world, were they only for my sake? Did I just want things to be easy for myself? Did I want to escape? The two of us were so intertwined, our lives by this point so intimately connected, that I couldn't survive the losing of him. I didn't know what was good for him, but neither, I thought, did he. I was lost, grasping on to anything I thought might haul us out. Every day I had pushed, changing tack, coming at things from a different angle, and still nothing had seemed to work, at least not permanently. I thought that I could read him – I thought I could tell when his mind was moving into its darker spaces, but I had been wrong before, and couldn't trust that I wouldn't be wrong again. Some hours,

I felt him – the old Elias – with me, but always we arrived back to this same point: him on the bed, staring into empty space, at something only he could see.

I looked across at him without speaking, trying to make out what he might be thinking. Always, I was trying to detect things in his eyes, his movements, his speech, trying to see if something was crystallising, if a new plan was forming. Was that a flicker of the old Elias, or a trick of the new one? I turned back to the book. The first poem I stopped at had a title whose grammar was easy enough to make out: '*Min ångest är en risig skog.*' My ... something is a ... something forest.

'Elias,' I called to him, '*vad menar "ångest"*'?

He looked up, slightly startled. Maybe he suspected that I was reading something about him, or about what had happened, as I had done in the past, trying to make some sense of it.

'Sorry. It's just in a poem,' I said, lifting the book so he could see it.

'Oh.' He turned over, wearily. 'Like when you're a teenager,' he said, 'and you're angry.'

Right. Perhaps that was it, but I wasn't sure, so I read him the whole line, testing its sound against the silence.

'*Min ångest är en risig skog.*'

He paused and thought for a second, and then said, '*Angst*. No, more like *anguish*. Or maybe *anxiety*. Something between those words, or all of them at once.'

'And what about *risig*?'

'*Worn out*,' he said.

I smiled at him. 'Yes. *My anguish ... is a worn-out forest.*' I said it aloud in English, and he looked up at me.

'*Ja*,' he said, smiling weakly back at me, and I held his

gaze for a moment before he put his head back down on to the pillow.

It was as though something beyond the words had been said between us, some other voice speaking in the room, and we had both heard it, and we had both understood. I pulled out a notebook and then the dictionary off the shelf, and wrote the line down: *My anguish is a worn-out forest*. I moved on to the next, and found I could make it out: *Where bleeding birds screech*. I thought it best not to say that aloud – the poem was getting darker than I hoped. As I moved through the two neat stanzas, crossing and re-writing and flicking through the dictionary, it was like uncovering something that had been lost to me, but then the more I worked, the more I found that I didn't want to know where it was going.

I reached the end, a stark, unrhymed finish.

> *Jag ligger snart still under tomma träd*
> *och ruttnar bland fågelliken.*

> Soon I will lie still under the empty trees
> and rot amongst the birds.

I looked over to check on Elias, uneasily, and closed the book, hoping he wouldn't ask me what I'd found.

Perhaps that was enough poetry for one day.

*

After a while, Elias seemed to have fallen asleep. I stood up and looked over at him, crumpled on top of the duvet, still in his jeans and sweater. I went into the kitchen and opened another beer, and lay back on the sofa, drinking it and staring at the ceiling. My mind was knotted and unclear. I couldn't tell whether it was an absence of thoughts, or too many thoughts at once. I couldn't pull any of the threads straight. Somehow, I was dulled by thinking, had thought so much that now all the thoughts had overrun each other, and what was left was a woolly, incessant muffle, a vague dread, a tangle of conflicting, overlapping inconclusiveness, and I hadn't got the energy to unravel it.

Whatever my mind had been filled with before, I could not recall. It was as though, looking into the dark, the dark itself had begun to move. The regions I had thought uninhabited were now beginning to rouse, the emptiness blooming into a hundred alien shapes. What before was transparent was now crawling, filling and overfilling so that the clear grammar of my thought was submerged by half-formed things. I closed my eyes, sick of myself, but I couldn't escape it. It wasn't that I remembered, but that I felt I was back there, physically, and it was all happening again. Elias, the pills, the phone-call. I felt a cold sweat spread along my back. But this time, when I opened my eyes, the images were not gone: I saw him in the kitchen, choking. I shook my head, and looked away, into the hall, and there he was, hanging from the doorframe.

Not real, I whispered. *Not real.*

He was on the bed. He was fast asleep.

I closed my eyes and breathed in deeply. But now, in the inescapable cinema of my skull, I saw myself: the same things were happening to me. It was *me* choking in the kitchen, *my* hand reaching into the knife drawer, me doing what Elias had never done. In there, behind my eyes, the real and unreal were overlaid, a loop of film projected and flickering over my vision, fading now, then clear again, as though my eyes were not closed at all.

Not real. Not real.

I don't remember how long I lay there, but when I woke up, it was past 3 a.m. The curtains were still open and the lights were on. I climbed into bed beside Elias and nuzzled my head into his side, but he didn't stir. The next day I was exhausted, and he was exhausted too, and as the days that followed passed by they seemed to slip in beside each other, blurring together. Still, time flowed outside the window, but not in here. We had made a capsule for ourselves, separate from the world. For weeks, Elias slept in the day time or watched television. Sometimes his parents would drive us over to the family home for dinner, or would come to the apartment, quite nervously, bringing food, both of them self-conscious, as if the flat were rigged with tripwires. I spent those weeks watching Elias, reading him for clues, and trying desperately to keep up with my work, reading, trying to write but struggling to focus. Hopkins, poetry, theology . . . Everything felt futile, seemed pointless.

I felt hounded and couldn't rest. Even in my sleep I was on the run, trying to catch Elias in time before he jumped from a building or drank a bottle of bleach, or kicked away the chair and left his feet kicking frantically in the empty air. I would find his body in swimming pools, slumped in bathrooms, choking on his tongue, and I would scream and cry and grab hold of his face, and then I would wake up, in shock, and see him sitting on the sofa, covered in his blanket, the glow of his laptop lighting his dull face blue.

In one recurring dream, I found Elias in a subaquatic forest, the tall fronds of kelp around us, and him tangled in a rope looped through a millstone. The water was still and thick, and no sound travelled through it. Sometimes I was walking on the seabed, and could feel the hard ridges of the sand beneath my soles. Other nights I was swimming, and was so cold I felt as though I were on fire. When I found Elias, his eyes were empty, as dead as sea glass, whitened over with cataracts. Because I was cold, I couldn't offer him my warmth, couldn't press myself to him, and because I knew somehow that my lungs were filled with water, I couldn't kiss him back to life. I sat on the sea floor and held his hand and cried beside him, watching the kelp forest sway above us, and, a mile above that, the light-ripples moving on the surface. I ran my fingers along the rill of his knuckles, as though it were a wishing stone, feeling the sun set on the world above us, and the water getting colder and darker.

Sometimes I would wake then, not knowing how the dream ended. Other times I would see a diver near the surface, his silhouette like an angel a mile above us, and then I noticed or knew somehow that it was myself, or some future version of myself that had come to tell me something, to save me, perhaps, to tell me a secret, to assure me that all of this would mean something in the end. I never met him or heard what he said, but I knew that was why he was there. Then, as the temperature dropped around me and I started to freeze, still holding Elias's hand, I broke at last through sleep and into the night-dark room, and each time Elias was sleeping beside me, and I would shake him awake, panicked, to make sure he was still alive.

Weeks went by and soon it was late November, and the days were a dull steel grey, full of a thick mist in the mornings, so in a way the whole world seemed as if it were sunk at the bottom of an ocean. What little light there was was smothered by the clouds, so that it reached the city dispersed and unsettled, as if from behind a screen. Gothenburg was quiet. When I left to go to the shop for food, the streets were eerily empty, only a few silent figures moving along the pavements in long coats and scarves: cones of lamplight, the lilting fog, the shapes of playgrounds and the shop signs, slow cars appearing out of the opaque air then disappearing again, swallowed down the white throat of the street.

Some days it felt like we were making progress, unknotting the threads, but then something would go wrong and I stopped out of fear that I would push him too far.

'You don't understand,' he would say, his eyes red with frustration, begging me.

And he was right: I didn't. And my not understanding made it worse. It reinforced his separateness, his isolation, and it reinforced mine, too. I tried, over and over again, and always our conversation fell apart, blistered into crying and shouting. He just needed to be listened to, to be heard, and I wanted to do that for him – I wanted to hear him – but that was easier said than done. If he said that the only way out was to kill himself, could I listen without saying no? If he began to spiral downwards, should I sit beside him or try to lift him up? It was unbearable to listen, unbearable to be passive when he was slipping away, unbearable to watch him drowning and not hold out my hand, not to take his, not try with all my strength to haul him back to the light.

*

The problem was that I still looked at things as though there were something to be fixed. I was desperate for it to be over. I was caught inside a nightmare with him, and thought that only he could let us out. For every worry, I looked frantically for an answer. For every one of Elias's thoughts, I looked for the opposing thought, the thing that might bring it into balance. I wore myself out with solutions, and it was months before I realised I was trying to fix something that couldn't be fixed. It wasn't that there was no hope of change or no hope of coming through to the other side. It wasn't that no solutions could be found to the things Elias worried about, but all of those things started deeper, in some impenetrable place, and it didn't matter if I attended to each one in turn. More of them would come, or the same ones would grow back. It took so long for me to learn that, and I know now how exhausting that must have been for him, how exhausting it must have been not to be understood, not to be heard, to have every question met with an answer.

Part of the problem was language itself, or what we were able to do with it. Ever since we met, Elias and I had had to translate ourselves to each other. From that first naming-game in the bar in Peru, and every day since. This seemed universal, in the sense that everyone has to translate when they try to bring something of themselves into language, hoping that the person listening might catch the sense of it, might see in the words a glimmer of the self who speaks them. Over time, I realised, I had worked out ways to simplify my speech, hoping that, in doing so, Elias might better understand me in his second language. But there was always the missing things, the less rounded edges of my thought that would be lost on the way. In simplifying my speech, I worried that I was simplifying what he could know of me, or that I was simplifying the ways in which he might know me. No doubt he was doing the same, but rather than simplifying himself in his own language, he was simplifying himself in mine. What he didn't have the word for, or the grammar for, had to be left unsaid. Maybe part of the problem, looking back, was here, in the things we lost between each other, in our failed sentences, in the things we lost the courage to say. In easier times, there was less at stake. What did it matter if a few things were lost, when we had so much in store? But soon the space between us became dark and impassable, and in the aftermath we had lost so much of ourselves that we hadn't the energy to try it all again.

What was left to Elias and I, after we'd exhausted ourselves, trying to dredge up words and failing, over and over again, were the words of others. The days came gloomily and unchanging. It was difficult even to say where one ended and the other started. One smeared into the next, the sun barely rising, the night always at hand, never leaving off completely. We stayed home and eventually a month had passed, and we were sealed off from the world. I tried to keep a routine at first: getting up early, making a pot of coffee and sitting at the table with my books spread around me and my laptop out. I burned candles in the morning, not wanting to wake Elias with the light, and tried to keep on top of work. I found whatever English books I could in the central library, or scrolled through e-books, losing my place often, my mind zoning out, my eyes aching. I read manuscripts online, folio after folio of diaries, sermons, letters, notebooks.

At some point, I lost track of how long we had been in that room together. My work became hermetic, detached, surreal. And, alongside my work on Hopkins, a different sort of work emerged. Just as we had done that first night, some afternoons and evenings I would lie on the sofa with a book of poems, my notebook open, the dictionary splayed across my lap. In the end, it was the little blue book, the poems of Karin Boye, that seemed to clarify things, to carry them over somehow. She lived with us those days, like a ghost cohabiting. In the evenings I would take up a book of poems and ask him to read lines, to translate words, to

explain bits of syntax, and together we would piece together
a voice in the space between us.

Before long we'd filled half a notebook with scribbled
translations. One word would proliferate into others, half a
dozen or more meanings or synonyms, none of them quite
right in English, none correlating exactly in their sounds or
associations, like a set of keys that didn't quite fit the lock.
Elias would list all the things each word reminded him of,
all the things each one meant, or could mean, in different
formulations, all the ways each one could carry a thought or
a feeling and mean something subtly different. Each line of
each poem would emerge slowly, changing shape as it
arrived, and between us we'd chisel it down to something
that suited us both, finding the right words, and trying to
keep the music of the language, which had a meaning of its
own, something that echoed beyond the words, and seemed
to catch a glimmer of the world behind them.

We struggled most over those which meant most, those
whose cadence and fragile thought seemed so carefully
made, so delicate, that taking it apart and putting it together
again risked the soul of it seeping out. One small poem was
crystal clear in the Swedish, but seemed to crumble in our
hands when we tried to lift it on to the new page. Looking
back at the notebook now, I can see the crossings-out, the
places where we'd had to find new words, the lines in which
English syntax was too loose, too long, for the original
thought. Karin Boye's poem is there, copied out on the left-
hand page of the notebook, neat and precise:

> *En stillhet vidgades mjuk som soliga vinterskogar.*
> *Hur blev min vilja viss och min väg mig underdånig?*
> *Jag bar i min hand en etsad skål av klingande glas.*

Då blev min fot så varsam och kommer inte att snava.
Då blev min hand så aktsam och kommer inte att darra.
Då blev jag överflödad och buren av styrkan ur sköra ting.

Then, pages and pages of our attempts. In the final version, the one we'd been happiest with, we wrote:

A stillness expanded, tender as a sunlit winter forest.
I wonder how I learnt to trust myself? How did I find
  my way?
I carried in my hand an etched bowl of ringing glass.

Then I walked gently, and would not stumble.
Then my hand was steadied, and would not shake.
Then, when I faltered, I was borne by the strength of a
  fragile thing.

It was the final line we couldn't get right. That was the line that changed often over the pages, crossed and re-crossed, the syntax all wrong, the meaning not quite there. The final line of the original has the speaker '*överflödad*', *over-flooded*, steadied by concentration, the fragility of the bowl coursing through her, holding her up. So she is 'borne' by the strength of something else, feels it moving through her body, and is changed by it. It was too much for me to get into English – the language didn't seem able to hold it.

There were many lines like this, many words and ideas we struggled to make new homes for. Slowly, each day, lines would emerge between us, with Karin as our intercessor. Each poem was like an icon, something we spoke through, something that seemed to crystallise our broken thoughts into forms we could both understand. They were like those

etched bowls of ringing glass – we carried them and they
steadied us; we let them course through us, feeling them re-
making us with their clarity. And in calling up those echoes
from another time, in sounding the darkness behind the
words for whatever might be found there, it was as though
we called something else up, too, a ghost to live between us,
someone to carry those fragile, shimmering parts of ourselves across to each other. Karin, carrying messages like
crystal bowls from one of us to the other. In her poems
there were woods, flowers bursting open, the deep, painful
recesses of a mind somehow brought on to the page, and
when the translation was finished, when we had decided on
which word went where, had fitted them together as best
we could, we read them aloud together and thought 'Yes.'
We thought, 'This is how it is. We are not alone after all.'

*

The morning was still dark, the ice brocaded along the edges
of the windows, and outside a thick fog was lilting between
the thin branches of the birches. The white of their bark was
lost in it, so only their arms, raised in the white sky, were
visible. They reached up out of the opaque air like children
asking to be carried off out of the cold. I was sitting at the
table, the coffee steaming in the pot. The candle on the windowsill was the brightest thing in the room, its tiny crocus
of flame flickering in the winter draught. Elias was on the
sofa, lying under a thick-knit blanket, watching TV on his
laptop. He was wearing his headphones, so the room was
hushed, only broken by the occasional guttering of the candle and the clunking of the central heating just starting to
waken.

I had taken a book about Karin Boye from the library on Avenyn, but after half an hour of trying to read the introduction, I had given up. Its academic language was impenetrable, stacked with words I didn't know. So far, the only thing I had managed to make out was the blurb on the back cover. Even there, I relied on simple phrases. *Born in Gothenburg in 1900. Died in Alingsås, 1941.* Alingsås ... I knew I recognised the name of the town, but I couldn't place it. Was it on the train route out of town? Or had I just seen it on a map somewhere, or heard it in conversation?

'Elias?'

He looked up, hearing me through the headphones, and took them off. 'Ah?'

'Where's Alingsås?'

He shook his head. I was hopeless, I knew. 'You've been there. With me. Don't you remember? The light festival?'

Of course. That was it. How could I have forgotten? We had gone there one night, back when Elias was still in hospital, after he was allowed to go outside accompanied. We drove there with his parents. It was a small town about thirty miles outside of Gothenburg, nestled between two lakes and surrounded by deep pine woods. There was a river.

'*Vad heter floden?*' I asked.

'Säveån.'

That was it, the name of the river. It flowed right through the town, between a cobbled embankment. I remembered it lit with lanterns, strung over with glowing orbs. I looked up the river online – its name came from *sæva*, meaning *calm* or *still*; and that was just it – the river moved quietly, slowly, with little in the way of current to swirl its black surface.

For the month of October, Alingsås put on a festival. As the nights came earlier and the darkness was more absolute, the town lit itself up. Strings of LEDs hung between the buildings, cables of red and orange in the forest paths, bright blue rods in the squares, branches up-lit by coloured spotlights, bulbs suspended over the water like a row of moons. As we had driven into the town, down the narrow streets, there were reams of people walking around, tucked up in ski jackets and woolly hats, drinking hot drinks from Styrofoam cups. We parked the car and got out. Elias had seemed calm and happy to be out of the hospital, glad of the fresh air.

Alingsås was quite far from home, so there was little worry that we'd meet anyone we knew, and besides it was dark between the lights and everyone was so wrapped up in their winter clothes that only the pale circles of their faces showed. Away from the main grid of the streets we walked out by the river and up into the woods, where the trees seemed almost inverted by the light, weird and monumental. The darkness was held at bay above us – if you looked up, you could see the blue hum of light over the town, like a force field, and then the blackness of the cold night vaulted above it. As we walked through the woods, everyone was whispering, as though each of them had learnt to preserve the peace, to give themselves over to looking and to thinking. Even the children spoke in hushes, grabbing on to their parents' trouser legs, or asking to be lifted on to shoulders, and staring up, wide-eyed, their faces softly coloured by the lights.

I remember that as we walked, Elias's father told me about a town in Norway, far north, which entered a period of total darkness for six months of each year. Because of the steep mountains that surrounded it, he said, when the sun was low in winter the light never reached down into the valley, and so the town lived in permanent night. I pictured the snow on the high peaks, the frozen waterfalls glinting on the mountains in the low, pink sun, and the people coming out of their houses each day and looking up, seeing the light high up above them, a warmth they longed to feel on their faces, but couldn't reach.

The town was built close to a waterfall, which generated electricity for a power plant, which in turn fed a fertiliser factory where the people of the town worked. After a few years, the owners worried that their workers weren't getting enough sun – they were gloomy, tired, claustrophobic. When the sun dropped and didn't come back for half a year, they fell out of sync with the world – they rose when the sun didn't, and went to bed having seen nothing but electric light. Their hormones were shaken up and disturbed. In the late 1920s, Elias's father said, a gondola was built above the town, and residents were transported up into the mountains where they could sit in the sunshine for a few hours, before travelling back into the valley. Still, that was only a small amount of light. Then, someone had an idea to build a *solspeil*. He said the word in Swedish.

'What's that?' I asked, not following. He translated it as a *sun mirror*.

Three huge moving panes were placed on the steep side of the mountain, tracking the sun and angling its rays down into the market square, where its ellipse was concentrated into a small pool of daytime. Elias's father told me he'd seen the people on television, smiling in the square, leaning back into the sun's warmth, cheering as the mirror caught the light and burned whitely, sending its gift down into the valley. I looked around myself at the children, bathing in the coloured lights under the trees, and the adults all whispering to each other, and Elias and his mother behind us, the reflections glistening in their eyes, watery with the cold.

I didn't see any sign of Karin Boye that night, but then again I wasn't looking for her, I didn't know her then. Getting up from the table, I handed one of the library books to Elias and he read the introduction to me, stopping and starting to gloss the phrases, to explain the meaning of some difficult words, his English stumbling in places when the writer used a technical phrase or a noun for something that had fallen out of use since the book was published: the strictures of Karin Boye's personal life were, at one point, compared to a mangle, and even though I knew what he meant when he explained, I had lost the English word for it, too. As we read through the introduction, the plain facts of Boye's life emerged in slow and devastating bluntness. It was in the woods around Alingsås that she had been found dead in late April 1941. Nearly a year before that day, she had taken a train from Stockholm, leaving her partner Margot, and travelled to Alingsås, where her friend Anita was dying. When she arrived and looked at Anita, she realised that she loved her. For Karin, the author said, love was like a moon, waxing and waning – sometimes her depression seemed to eclipse it, other times it seemed to brighten it through the sheer force of contrast. One phrase in particular struck me: her mother said that, when Karin was with Anita in Alingsås, she seemed to split herself in two.

Anita worked for a psychoanalyst, Iwan Bratt, and Karin stayed as a guest at his home. It was surrounded by chestnut trees, and Iwan used to sit some evenings outside, playing a lute, its notes echoing through the branches and heard through the windows of the two-storey wooden house where Karin sat down to write. One day Karin walked into the backroom of the local pharmacy, opened a bottle of sleeping pills, and poured them into a paper cone. She took a bottle of

Vichy water, too. In the foyer of the pharmacy, though, she froze and dropped the bottle and the pills to the floor. As Elias read the passage, I could see all those bright coloured pills spilling around her feet, and began to tense up, sensing a too-close parallel emerging, an unexpected, revisited trauma. The thought of suicide was running through Karin's mind, overwhelming it, but she held it back. Still, it would not stop haunting her. I heard Elias's voice start to shake.

'It's OK,' I said, placing my hand on the book and closing it to stop him from reading. He let me, and I put the book down on the table and took his hand in mine, stroking my thumb across his.

This story made sense now, after all our weeks of reading her poems. There were dark things in those poems, things I'd never quite pieced together, which her biography brought into a new clarity. In a late poem, one I had read late one night while Elias was asleep, she wrote:

> *Lyssnar jag, hör jag livet fly*
> *ständigt snabbare nu.*
> *De lugna stegen bakom –*
> *död, det är du.*

> I listen, I hear life fleeing
> steadily faster now.
> The calm steps behind me –
> death, it is you.

I remembered my feeling that Elias was being stalked, followed by another person who wanted to kill him. '*Död, det är du.*' 'Death, it is you.' And all the time I was scared he would give in, would let himself be taken, and I couldn't trust him to leave my sight. He was followed all the time by that other self, that anti-self who showed in the empty pools of his eyes, his thinning frame.

Det är som du ville mig något.
En gåva vill du visst ha:
en underlig liten nyckel –
det lilla ordet ja.

It is as though you want something from me.
A present, that's what you want:
A curious little key –
That little word, 'yes'.

On 23 April 1941 Karin went out to the woods to meet that other self. Perhaps not far from where Elias and I had walked that evening. Every day, every night, I was afraid of him doing the same: turning around, looking into the face of death, and saying that little word, 'yes'.

On that day, Karin had an argument with Anita – something about the cinema, some film they had wanted to see – and she had walked home and had gone into the kitchen. The housemaid, Märta, was washing pots at the sink. I can see Karin now, just under five feet tall, standing in the kitchen, a slant of afternoon sun spreading across the floor, throwing a hoop of amber light over the breakfast table. She's by the doorway in her grey hat, black skirt and small flat black shoes, wringing her handkerchief, twisting it into a rope, knotting it around her fingers, then pulling each one free. She lifts up her blue eyes and asks Märta what time it is, as casual as anything, and Märta tells her – twenty past one – and the next moment, when Märta turns around, Karin is gone.

The police report was dated 28 April, five days after she went missing. The search parties came out in force – the military, the police, the public – and then a call came from a local man who had found her, curled up on the floor, no more than 300 metres into the woods outside the town. She had two empty bottles by her side: one of Vichy water, another which had carried the sleeping pills. Her body was taken to Stockholm, where she was buried in early May. At the end of that month, Boye's partner Margot gassed herself in her apartment. Ten weeks after that, Anita died in a hospital in Malmö. The Swedish poet Gunnar Ekelöf said, 'It's like in Shakespeare. All of them are dead.'

*

I took the books back to the library the next morning. They felt dangerous, too close to home, as though somehow they had scripted our life before we had lived it. Still, after that night, the psychic toll of those stories, and our own, began to haunt us in new and more oblique ways. Each morning we woke more and more tired. It was as though we were wearing ourselves out in our sleep, thrashing through water, on the run. The more questions Elias asked, the more their hooks lodged in my mind and I couldn't shake free of them. I began to grind my teeth so hard that one morning I woke up with one of my molars broken in two. I lifted the shard of it out with my fingers and held it up. It was like something carried through from the dream, evidence that it was real after all.

After that first month of living in our flat together, seeing no one, I began to trust Elias enough that I would walk outside when he was asleep. I would leave the house and try to pull my mind back together again, wandering for hours, as though the paths might help me to unravel the knotted mess of the story, to find the sense in it. Not wanting Elias to know, I had stowed away some beers and bottles of gin in the basement storage of the apartment, and before I left the building I would go down and get some and walk out with the bottle. I needed that daze, that dulling which seemed to level things, to unravel me. Most nights I couldn't fall asleep at all unless I was half-drunk.

For most of my life I had thought that all I could be sure of was the past. I think I had seen memory as a sort of route, a pathway, which stopped off at all the significant events of my life, and formed a narrative, explaining how I got to where I am, and how I got to be who I am. Like stepping stones across the river Lethe, there were some memories I held on to. Over all that river of forgetfulness – into which experiences, thoughts and words dropped every day – these memories made a crossing, some solid ground I could traverse. All those years, it was as though time were blowing through me and taking form, being winnowed into narrative.

After Elias took himself to the summerhouse that day, I had felt the ground beneath me, all the imagined certainty of that narrative, blasted apart. And as I stood in the aftermath, the safest thing to do seemed to be to stop acknowledging the flow of time, to look anywhere but forward. I arrested everything into an endless, enduring present: the idea that time would progress, would alter, seemed impossible. If I acknowledged the possibility of a future, I acknowledged the possibility of Elias's death – of his leaving, of my own death, or of my own life without him – and so I shut out time altogether. I didn't dare to ask for the future. I could not tell what the past would be made of next. So each night

I walked out into the mist or the rain or the freezing stillness of the woods. I sat on benches and drank. I smoked
cigarette after cigarette until my hands were too cold to
hold them. I ghosted myself, pulled myself outside of time,
walked at night in a place where no one knew me, and pretended, in that way, that I did not exist.

*

I could not talk about what had happened. The gulf of
experience seemed impassable. I called my mother or my
father most days, sometimes more than once a day, but
otherwise it was just me and Elias. I think that, too, is why I
walked out each night after he had fallen asleep. I would
quietly walk into the hallway and put on my boots, take
down my long woollen coat, my scarf, and wrap myself up
for the icy world outside. I had lost my trust, my sense of
certainty in him, but when he slept he rarely woke for hours,
and I knew I could leave the house and come back before he
knew I'd been away. So most nights I took the chance to
wander the streets of the city alone, my ears burnt red from
the cold, my breath pluming up into the autumn fogs. As the
heavy main door closed behind me and I stood on the top of
the hill, the lights of the city sparkled below me like an
inverted star-scape. I could hear the faint jingle of tram-bells
down at the crossroads, and the deeper silence of the park
and the woods to the north. The anonymity of night-time
was what I needed – I wanted to be unseen, to be absent.

Apart from by the road, the building was also accessible by
a woodland path that linked the suburbs of the city together
and formed a ring around the main streets. That path at night
was lit by a line of lamps, with long stretches of blackness

between them. Every so often the path would emerge out into a street, or into a park amongst tall buildings and shops, and then it would disappear again into thick, stripped woods of oak and silver birch, a worn-out forest of my own. One night, though, I took a different route, almost by instinct, turning off the path and down to the park. Perhaps I had the echo of our translations in my mind, and the echo carried me, or called me in search of another ghost. The first night I did it, it happened almost by chance, though I think I knew where I was going all along. We had been reading Karin Boye again, and I must have been thinking of her, hearing her speaking as I walked down along the mud-path through the leafless trees on the hill, into the park where the pond was making soft noises under the wet feathers of the sleet.

As I passed it and then came out on to the central avenue, the flakes were thick and sweeping, melting to water as they hit the windscreens of the cars, running down the glass in thick veins of light. People walked with their umbrellas snapping backwards in the wind, or huddled under the awnings of the restaurants, peering out into the street, chattering, pointing like children at the sheer white downpour. As I passed, the red lamps above the cinema porch unspooled like fires. I ducked into a 7/11 to buy another pack of cigarettes, my wet shoes squeaking on the linoleum floor, the front of my thighs dark with water. I shook myself, and could feel that my legs were frozen beneath my jeans, so I stood around, pretending to browse the magazines beneath where the air-conditioner was blowing, my face red, my lips chapped with the cold. I took off my headphones and listened as the sleet turned to rain. The droplets were so heavy that they splashed inside the shop, and the faulty automatic doors kept sliding shut, hesitating midway and then opening again. In the security camera I saw myself standing there: a phantom, drenched in my long coat, opening another packet of cigarettes, my fingers numb.

The rain eased slightly, and was gentle enough now to begin sweeping in the squalls of wind coming down the avenue from the direction of the harbour. I stepped outside again and stood under the uncertain shelter of the building where the sprays of weather only occasionally reached. Slipping off my right glove, I took out a cigarette, balancing it between my lips while I rooted around in the inside pocket of my coat. Even the metal grooves in the lighter hurt my thumb when I tried to strike the flint inside, and when it worked the flame was a low, lethargic thing, so I had to turn my back to the street and lean against the wall to keep it alive. I breathed in a few short breaths, trying to draw the flame, and when the tobacco caught there was the familiar hushed crackling noise as the smoke drew upwards, and the deep, soothing heaviness as the smoke settled in my lungs, my head fizzing slightly as I drew it in.

I put the lighter away, held the cigarette bobbing on my bottom lip, while I put my glove back on, the smoke getting in my eyes, and then took it again between two woolly fingers. Again, the rain slowed, and the sky seemed to brighten slightly this time, as though it were finally reaching its old clarity, the clouds being thinned and swept off by the wind, revealing a little cavern of high silver where the moon was beaming through.

I flipped the heavy collar of my coat upwards and hunched myself slightly as I walked, trying to keep warm, and as I took my careful steps along the wet road towards the library, I noticed out of the corner of my eye a woman standing alone, completely still, staring out at the few passers-by. Because of how my scarf and collar were up around my throat and chin, I had to turn my whole body to look at her, and when I did I found myself standing face to face not with a woman – or not with a living woman – but with a statue.

She was small, slight, and wore a simple smock-dress. Her bronze face was set under a neat bob of hair, and though her chin was lifted slightly, almost defiantly, her blank eyes didn't look down at me, but looked outwards, softly, almost sadly, so she had a slightly contradictory air both of resignation and determination. And it was strange – there was no eye-contact, and no possibility of imagining it – but still I was sure, in that moment, that she knew I was there. She avoided my gaze, but I knew she had seen me, or that she felt me watching.

The night was already brutally cold and she was wet with rain. It would probably freeze by morning. I pictured the frost lacing itself over her face like a white veil. And then I noticed, in her hand, a clipped rose, placed by someone between her fingers and her palm. Someone, still, was mourning her. I looked around for an inscription, but found none. And then it clicked: she was standing by the library, this small, defiant woman. Her features matched the descriptions Elias had read to me. *Karin*, I whispered. *It must be you.*

I took another drag of my cigarette, and watched the end blister red, and felt its brief heat as it shrunk down towards the filter. *Just me and you*, I thought, looking at her, the two of us out here in the night with nowhere to go. Karin, Karin, Karin. I spun the 'r' out, trilling it softly on my tongue. Her name: the long vowel of it, then the swift, clipped ending. Open, then closed. My mouth moved around it, made it, finished it, over and over, as though it might teach me something, a prayer with no hope of an answer. I almost raised my hand to her as I turned back to face the street, the traffic, the hill tall and dark with trees, not wanting to leave abruptly, or to say goodbye without saying goodbye.

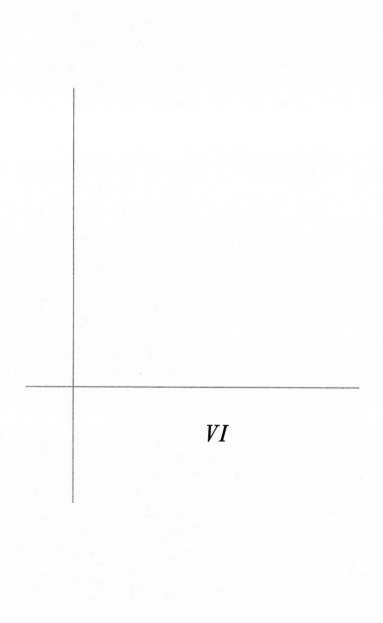

VI

I remember the first time he said it. At the end of an argument, one evening, Elias, slumped at the foot of the bed: 'If you leave me, I'll have nothing left. If you go, that will be the end.' Perhaps it was meant as a sign of love, but it didn't feel like it. I stared at him, shocked that he had said the words. His final, desperate hand laid down. If I left, he would kill himself. I didn't know how to react.

'You can't say that,' I told him. 'Don't. Please.'

I started to cry, holding his arm. I looked at him in horror, not just at what he might do to himself, but at what he would do to me. He held my life, my hopes, my love, in his body. I couldn't take the weight of it. I could feel it like a stone-press pushing down on my chest. He was helpless, and now, I thought, he would make sure I was helpless, too. He felt out of control, and he looked around and his eyes lighted on me.

Of course, there were days when I wanted to cut and run. Sometimes it was my conscience, sometimes it was love, but whatever it was, something always tugged at the leash, always brought me back. A twitch upon the thread. Now, though, I felt that the choice was no longer my own. If things turned, if something happened, it would be my fault for not stopping it, my fault for giving up. At first, selfishly,

I couldn't understand that my love wasn't strong enough to keep him from the brink. I thought it must be weak or defective. Surely if I loved him properly, he wouldn't be prepared to give himself up. Now everything was reversed: he looked at me and asked me to prove it.

And so, a new note was struck – a constant echoing reminder, a warning that kept me in line. I was told not to tell anyone about what had happened, especially not my friends. To protect Elias, to protect myself from more of what I could not take, I agreed. My parents, of course, already knew. I had called them on the day of his birthday – I couldn't backtrack on that. Likewise, I had called one friend at home. Everyone else, though, would have to be kept in the dark. I tied myself up in excuses when they asked why I couldn't come home. I told them everything was going well, or avoided telling them anything at all. For some more distant friends, that mattered less. For others, it meant I had to keep them at bay. I stopped calling them or stopped answering their calls. I isolated myself, following Elias's mantra that only in isolation could I keep him safe.

There is no morality to depression, no way to apportion blame for what either of us did, but every day I felt that weight crushing down on me, tightening my lungs, making my breaths quick and shallow. I felt that everything was to be given away; that nothing was my own. If I was to save him, I needed to be a non-person, to subsume myself; and if I broke – if I told someone, or if I seemed to be on the verge of leaving, caring too much for myself and not enough for him – I felt that threat rising through the room. I would be abandoning him. I would be confirming all of his darker suppositions. Any wrong turn might lead to disaster. Not for the first time, I had to displace myself from myself. Not for the first time, I found myself caught inside a secret.

*

In the first weekend of December a few friends I had known since university came over from London to Gothenburg. They had never managed to come up to Liverpool when we lived there, and had never met Elias. They were eager to know who this handsome man was. They wanted to meet him. We had arranged the trip months before, and I had forgotten about it until it was too late to cancel. Elias didn't want them to know anything was wrong, so I let them come and told them nothing. They had been supposed to stay at our flat – on the sofa, on the floor – and just the thought of them all living with us, if only for a weekend, was insurmountable. There was no way we could cover up the truth for that long. I made up an excuse – the flat was being redecorated – and they booked a hotel near Järntorget, far enough away from us that Elias felt safe.

Those wintery days, the town took on the atmosphere of a film noir, a time of blackout and hushed conspiracy. There was snow, too, and the narrow, unsalted paths were slippery, smeared with old leaves. I met my friends as they got off the airport bus, and had to tell them that Elias was feeling unwell – a stomach bug, I think – and they sighed, collectively disappointed, hoping he'd get better soon. I clenched at the sentiment.

Elias's parents had agreed to go over to the flat after work to check in on him, and maybe have dinner together. I knew he would be alone only for a few hours before they arrived, but I had made Elias promise, holding my hand and looking into my eyes, that he wouldn't do anything while I was away. I found myself checking the flat before I left. I took the packets of paracetamol from the bathroom cabinet and stashed them in a shoebox in the hallway while he wasn't looking. I took the razor from the bathroom, too, slipping out the blades carefully, wrapping them in tissue, and putting them into the inside pocket of my coat. There were things I couldn't take with me, though: the kitchen knives, the belts, the electric cables.

While I walked down the street, my friends chatting away about the flight, I was torn, unable to concentrate, struggling to pull my face into anything resembling a smile. They asked about my work, about the nightlife in the city, and I made things up as I went, pretending I was happy, and that nothing was wrong. We went towards their hotel, dragging suitcases through the mulch of the snow. The wheels were clogging up, so after only a few minutes we hoisted the cases up between us and carried them like boxes through the streets, along the cobblestones and the tram-tracks, and all the way I did my best to perform for them, trapped in the fiction I had invented.

The nights began now at about half-past three in the afternoon, so the light faded quickly as we walked, and the streets began to glow with the windows of the shops, and the bulbs of the trams shuttling along beside us. In Gothenburg, night seemed to happen in one of two ways. Sometimes, when the sky was clear, it was sudden, and seemed to fall vertically through the streets and between the buildings, like a guillotine dropping into a block. Other times, on misty days like this one, the air turned on itself, bruising, almost imperceptible, so gradual that the day would almost bleed into dark. I remember, on that evening, the dark seemed to move in stealthily, almost as if it were following us down the streets, and the streetlights flickered on as we walked, and my friends were giddy with it, with all the lights and the biting cold, so different to the London they had left just a few hours ago. I tried to see it with their eyes, and they were right: it was beautiful. I had forgotten that.

After they had checked into the hotel and had time to get into warmer clothes, we walked down to the old town, catching up about work and old friends along the way, and I almost managed to forget about my new life here, to slip back into the old one, and to pretend, even to myself, that everything was all right. In Haga we sat inside a café, sharing cardamom buns, and then we took the tram across town to Liseberg, a theme park in the city that was open at night in the winter, and was full of children running around under the coloured lights, or standing behind their fathers at shooting galleries, where massive bars of chocolate were ranged as prizes under the glass counters. We got mugs of mulled wine and I made my friends try salted liquorice, laughing as they winced, their eyes puckering at the taste. After the wine had warmed us, we went over to the ice rink, borrowed some skates, and made loose, uncertain laps of it. From the rink, you could look up to the hills and make out the apartment buildings ranged along them.

Skating over to the side of the rink, while the others were trying to skate backwards, clinging on to each other and laughing, I thought of our flat, up on the hill, behind the trees, and of Elias up there on his own. At least, I hoped that was where he was. How could I be sure? The longer I stood there, the more I began to feel a hot, sickening guilt flooding through me, draining the colour from my face. What was I doing down here, skating, tipsy on mulled wine, while he was up there on his own? Was this a test, and had I failed? I felt trapped, stuck on the rink with the stupid ice skates on, far away from him. What was I doing? How could I live with myself if something happened? I stood, clinging on to the side of the rink, watching the lights whirl to the heavy pop music, the people laughing. Then, almost as if I had willed it, or predicted it, I felt my phone starting to buzz in my pocket.

It was like I was back in a nightmare, like time was repeating, an endless loop I couldn't tear my way out of. I pulled off my glove with my teeth, dropped it on the ice, and wrangled my phone from my jeans pocket. It wasn't Elias's name on the screen, but his mother's, and for a moment I thought that this was it, that she'd turned up at the flat and found him dead, and it was all my fault. All this because I hadn't been brave enough to tell my friends the truth.

'*Hej*, Seán'.

'*Hej. Hur gå det?*' I asked, trying to seem calm.

'It's OK', she said. Then paused, and sighed. 'It's Elias. He won't open the door.'

'What do you mean, he won't open the door? Is he inside? Can you see him?'

'*Ja.*'

'Is . . . is he OK?'

'He says he doesn't want us to come in.'

In the confusion of the moment, I couldn't piece together what I was being told. I saw the pills, the screaming, the panic. Here I was again, surrounded by people, pretending that nothing was wrong. I was still pretending, still locked into my own silence. Still, I couldn't ask for help. There were my friends, waving at me, calling me over, and I smiled at them and pretended everything was OK.

'So he answered the door?' I asked, hurriedly, trying to make sense of it.

'No. We called him when he didn't open the door, and he said he was inside, but didn't want us to come in.'

I looked up at the hill and could picture his parents there, outside the apartment building in the cold, with bags of food for dinner, just wanting to see their son.

'I'll call him. *Oroa dig inte.* Don't worry. I'm sure it's OK.'

I hung up the phone, my hands shaking. Elias answered after a few rings.

'I'm *fine*,' he said, almost pleading, and I could hear something desperate, something trapped, like that voice he had spoken with on the phone the last time. 'Please. I want to be left alone. I need to be alone.'

Maybe that was all. Could we not just leave him in peace? But still, still, the doubt pressed on me, wouldn't let me go. The things Elias and I wanted seemed impossible to overlap. Thrown into constant anxiety, I tried and tried to let him out of my sight, but every time I did, I felt this seething fear. Elias, on the other hand, needed space, needed time to come to terms with himself. I wanted to give him that space, but in moments like this my instinct was to run to him, and I couldn't override it. Panicking, I told my friends that Elias had locked himself out and I needed to go home to let him back inside. They looked confused – not affronted, but somehow pitying, as though they could read my insincerity, or could see a panic in my eyes and knew I was covering something up. Pulling off my ice skates and stepping on to the cold, damp rubber floor around the rink, I told them I would meet them in the morning.

I was panicking, yes, but this time there was a rise of anger, too. I couldn't even leave the flat for a few hours without being called back. He was in charge. I was tied to the flat, to him, and I couldn't get free. I wanted desperately to escape – to get outside of life, outside of the apartment, outside of myself. I had lied to them; and now, running home, I was getting ready to lie again, steadying myself, not wanting to meet Elias with anger, but with comfort, and with calm. I was sick of it, sick of corralling my emotions back into my body, sick of all this hiding. As I walked up the hill, panting, I could feel something inside myself, and I didn't know if it was rage or grief or despair. It was some wild, formless thing, splitting out inside me. All my energy was sparking against my skin. My chest was sore, my hands flaring red. I wanted to smash something. I was so full of anger, so full of this frantic energy that my fists were clenching involuntarily. I couldn't show it to Elias. I couldn't show it to my friends. I was alone in it. My breath was caught, and at some point, running up the hill, I thought I might throw up. It felt like I had a muscle lodged in my throat, and I thought I would choke, and part of me wanted to choke. I swore, over and over again, cursing myself, cursing I didn't know what – the world, Elias, the whole fucking thing. I wanted to tear it all down, and I wanted to tear myself down with it.

*

Lying is something I had become good at with practice. Before I came out, it was so deeply integral to the way I lived my life that it was hard, afterwards, to unpick which parts of myself were armour and which parts of myself were real. For years and years, I curated my mannerisms, my hobbies, my taste in music, books, friends, clothes, haircuts.

Every extrinsic thing became an opportunity for diversion, a way to deflect any chance that people might see the part of myself I was keeping hidden. In fact, I'm not sure I ever outgrew that armour. Queerness involved a process of *becoming*, undertaken in a world built around heterosexuality, and so that process happened in no small part through the ways I butted up against the world I lived in. Sexuality was constructed into selfhood, into identity, as I grew up. I moulded myself in contrast to – or in consonance with – the world as I found it; I regulated myself, I policed myself.

When I read Karin Boye's letters, the dictionary splayed over my lap, I saw myself there. To a friend, she wrote that 'within everything I had made mine *from without, without it being mine*, there was a reality that *conflicted* with this outward self, beautiful but not my own.' All her religious and moral ideas, all the conventions she had brought inside herself, were at odds with another self she knew existed. 'There has been a hard battle within me,' she wrote, 'whether to give up my will or to worship my will.' To submit, or to assert. To have the freedom of invisibility, or the freedom of distinction. I had chosen to hide. I had lived a dual life, disconnected from my real self, so that by the time I emerged into adulthood, I was left with a task of rediscovery – or recovery. The trajectory was not always linear. If I was to move forward, to trade the freedom of invisibility for the freedom of distinction, I had to look back. I dug at the detritus of the years, brushed and dusted them away, and hoped that, in the end, I might find something intact, a part of myself preserved, brought up to the light.

Of course, it wasn't easy. The lies had become part of me, and some of the things I had suppressed never seemed to come back, or else they came back brutalised and changed.

Mostly, I found that the world outside the closet required me to keep the armour on. I traded my first closet for a bigger, roomier one. At work or at home, on public transport or just walking down the street, I shifted in and out of sight, always aware of being watched. I had practised secrecy for so long that I not only became adept at it, but it became part of myself, so that even walking down the street holding hands with another man seemed (in a contorted way) to be a violation not of the outside world, but of my own being. All those years spent sneaking around, littering my path with a thousand white lies, left me reluctant to be found out, scared of betraying myself.

As a child I was a famously good liar. My mother, who was a primary school teacher when I was growing up, said that out of all the children she knew, I was one of the few who could fool her completely. I would lie and I would believe the lie. I spent many hours observing the people around me to figure out what 'normal' looked like. Then, like a finely prepared actor, I stepped out and played the role. I got so good at it, in fact, that after a time even I started to forget which parts of myself were scripted and which parts weren't. Where did the character end and where did I begin? *How can we know the dancer from the dance?*

This set me in good stead for being a teenager. All teenagers get used to lying – they keep secrets, nurse private longings, and lash out when they find themselves treated, inexplicably, like children. They spend their days living in a halfway house between childhood and the adult world. But for me, the divide was even closer to home. I didn't just keep secrets from my family, but from my friends and, often enough, from myself as well. Following suit, I didn't just lash out at others, I lashed out at myself. When the real, buried part of me reared its head, I tried to push it down into the dark again, only to have its urgency up-end me.

Sometimes, when I felt that my grip on the lie was subsiding, or it seemed as though my carefully constructed other self was fading away, and my real self becoming too visible, too open to suspicion, I would take action. At high school, I started to spread rumours about myself, confiding in some loose-lipped friend that I fancied a girl in the year above, or insinuating that I had kissed someone at the disco that happened once a term at the local rugby club. When I was about fifteen years old, though, my fictions became more untenable. Quite quickly, people at school began to rack up notches on their bedposts (or notches on the benches of public parks), and still there I was, failing to take up any opportunity that presented itself. So, inevitably, the questions came. And when I felt close to detection, when groups of boys at school began calling me queer, naming the thing they had been honed to recognise, I hatched a plan.

When my parents were out one evening, and my brothers were not at home, I went down to the living room and turned on the television. It was a new wide-screen, and you could see it through the front window from the pavement across the street. In the evenings I would walk home and see the teatime soap operas playing, the backs of my family's heads turned towards the TV, watching. We lived on a main road – there were always cars going by, and kids from school walking along the street outside, waving over the hedge as they passed – and tonight, I hoped, would be no different. I drew open the curtains, looping the cord in a figure-of-eight on to the little cleat hook, and sat down on the sofa.

There were pay-per-view channels on the new TV. I had found them a few digits down from the music stations. On those channels, half-naked women flirted with the camera, sitting on plush red cushions, the chatline numbers panning across the lower part of the screen. I turned on the TV and found the right station. A woman called Sophie was lying in a blue bikini, her legs wrapped around a metal pole. I muted the volume, not wanting to hear the things she might say when a call came in, and I sat on the sofa with the big windows behind me and the noises of the cars passing, and I waited to be caught. My knees were shaking, as if I were very cold, and I put my hands on top of them to hold them down.

I don't know how long I sat there. I was afraid that my parents or my brothers would come home early, but perhaps that wouldn't be so bad after all. Perhaps that would buy me more time. Sophie began to move up and down the pole, holding onto it with her thighs, her long blonde hair tumbling over her shoulders. Then, after what felt like forever, I heard some shouts from outside, coming closer to the house. After a minute, the shouts burst into a cackle of excitement behind me. Then, there was a rapid banging on the window.

I jumped up, embarrassed now, not wanting to turn around. I could hear voices saying my name and laughing manically. When I finally turned my head, I saw them: three boys I knew from school, their breath smeared on the window. I stood staring at them, my face bright red. The reflection of the woman on the TV was projected across their faces, and the flats of their palms were pressed up on the glass like clammy stars. The woman's reflected dance moved across the pane, and I was completely still, frozen in place, as though I was caught inside the box of a camera, the only unmoving thing in a world of colour. I could hear them laughing in disbelief, jubilant at my shame, their words pealing down a scale like church bells, repeating, saying 'Oh my God', 'Oh my God', 'Oh my God'.

*

In my teenage years I spent my life in constant negotiation between these two selves. My real self was in there, but I only let him out on occasion, often when I was alone or when I was with people whose anonymity made them safe. At that time there were no other gay people (that I knew of) in my school of over 2,000 students. Clearly, there were kids performing their own works of legerdemain, hiding behind facades so carefully constructed that even I – a close observer of the art of deception – couldn't see past them.

I knew that I would have to look further afield. Online, I joined chat rooms or dating sites under false names, and invented detailed backstories about myself so that I couldn't be recognised. I split myself so many times that I lived out entire fantasies of imagined possibility in my mind, and in the minds of the men I spoke to. Occasionally, I was brave enough to broach the prospect of moving those imagined selves out of the internet and into real life. Sometimes, I arranged to meet people, but in the end I could never pluck up the courage to follow through. I left one boy, just a year older than me, waiting at a train station for over an hour, until he realised I wasn't coming, and sent me a heartbroken message when he got home. I felt guilty and ashamed.

Those fictional versions of myself were, paradoxically, closer to the real me than the me I showed to my friends and family, though each of them had a flourish of fantasy: a name I thought was more masculine than my own, perhaps. I was

John or Steve or Adam. Some of them had an interest in football (the details of which I gleaned through overhearing the talk of my brother when he watched the matches); others had secret girlfriends and were curious about being with men (a projection, probably, of my own fantasies about seducing the boys at school who made life hard for me).

At home, at night in my bedroom, I also experimented with lying to myself. I would close my eyes and bring into my mind the image of a girl from school, or a woman I had seen on television, and concentrate on the image, hoping to train myself into attraction. For months I attended to this personal conversion, thinking of men, longing for them, and then at the last minute substituting the image of a woman. I hoped that I might trick my body, might reset its desires if I could associate its pleasure with these imagined women. Each night, I communed with these women, feeling guilty for subjecting them to my experiments, exasperated at myself for not being able to hold their images in place. Unfailingly, my mind would revert. I would be focusing on their hair, their skin, the shape of their breasts – all those things the other boys talked about – but as I got closer to the edge of myself, a man would appear somewhere in the scene behind her and steal my attention.

Each night for months I practised this therapy, this ritual conditioning. After a time, I gave up. The power of these imagined people wore off, and I grew tired of the same shapes, the same smiles, the same places. I had so few images I could draw on: only once or twice had I seen another boy's body, and then only in glimpses, stolen in changing rooms or at sleepovers. If I saw a music video on the TV, or could make out the shape underneath a footballer's shorts, I would focus on it, memorise it, archive it for when I was next alone. My imagination lived on images, and even my fantasy worlds were made up of constructions and collages of reality. In the time of dial-up internet and a family computer that took several long minutes to download a single photograph, I had hardly any pictures to use. If, going about my life, I happened upon one, I would seize it, obsess over it, gaze at it like a talisman, hour by hour, until eventually it became faded and tawdry and lost its power.

So, starved and depleted and driven to invention, I turned to the one repository of images I had access to: those of my own body. Looking in the mirror, positioning myself so that my face wasn't reflected back at me, I would focus on a part of my body and imagine it to be the body of some other man. In that way, I came to know my body in two separate ways, both as the thing I lived inside and also as a thing very close to what I desired in other men. But this was never narcissistic; in fact, I had to focus intently on the body I was looking at *not being mine*. Those nights, I would lie in bed, or sit on the floor of my room, and look at portions of myself in the mirror and pretend they belonged to someone else. A strange mixture of isolation and communion, a perfect circle of loneliness and also a perfect circle of self-love, each overlapping, blending, so that for a while (though not a long while) I managed to be almost self-sufficient in my desire for other men.

Eventually, though, I realised that it wasn't only sex, but romance I wanted, in all its idealistic teenage frenzy. I wanted things I couldn't give to myself: the tension when my arm would brush against the arm of another, the shortness of breath I felt when a boy at school would, however accidentally, touch me. So I went back to the computer, took out one of my alter egos, and began talking to a boy who lived in a town not far from mine. This time I followed through and arranged to meet him at Piccadilly Station in Manchester the next weekend. We planned to go to a matinee at the Cornerhouse, which would give us time to get home afterwards, but also (I hoped) a place where we might sit in the dark together, away from the gaze of other people. Where I lived, the public transport was clunky and unreliable. A twenty-mile trip could take upwards of two hours. One bus, another bus, the rain streaming down the window, hurtling down the narrow lanes, and then the orderly brightness of the tram, its smooth slow journey through the suburbs and into the city. Even though it wasn't far, going into Manchester would mean being away from home all day.

When I reached Piccadilly, I was damp from the rain. My T-shirt stuck to my back and I could taste the wax from my hair as the water dripped down my forehead and nose and on to the top of my lip. I wanted time to sort myself out, to get dry, to check myself in the mirror before I met him. I took off my wet jacket and shook it out behind the sliding doors, the wind squalling into the station behind me – and then I saw him, standing by the departure boards. Tall, younger-looking than I expected, not at all dishevelled by the weather. I wondered if I could walk past him and take time to fix myself up before I said hello, but he noticed me staring and looked over quizzically, perhaps not knowing if it was me or not. I did a half-wave and a nod in his direction, before walking self-consciously across the wet linoleum of the station floor towards him. We shook hands awkwardly and he smiled as he introduced himself, then chattered nervously about the journey and the weather and how his hair was ruined. I ran my hand through my own hair to show him how wet it was, laughing, and told him I was just about to go to the bathroom to dry myself off.

We walked together across the concourse over to the toilets, where people were clumsily dropping change into the slots of the turnstiles and hobbling through, swinging their bags and coats behind them. I took out some coins from my pocket and went into the men's bathrooms on the left. When I came out again, a few minutes later, he was waiting for me and looked anxious and apologetic.

'Everything OK?' I asked.

'Sorry, I wanted to, but I didn't have any change.'

I looked at him, confused.

'You need money to get in. I couldn't come in after you.'

I thought he needed to go to the toilet, too, and said I had some spare coins, rooting my finger down into the leather flap of my wallet.

'No, it's OK,' he said, 'it doesn't matter.'

It was only months later that I realised what had happened in those awkward moments outside the station bathrooms. He had thought I was asking him to follow me, to come into the toilets, to have sex in the cubicle, and was embarrassed that he couldn't get through the turnstile. Though I didn't recognise it then, it was my first glimpse of that coded world I was about to be initiated into without my knowing.

*

At the time I thought it was probable that I was the only boy of my sort in my school. The bigger cities were far enough away to require a day trip, and besides, I didn't know anyone there anyway. There was no one around me I could ever hope would reciprocate. I was so full of longing that I didn't know how I could survive if I didn't get it out. There were straight boys at school who I wanted, who I dreamt of. I would get a thrill of excitement when they did so much as acknowledge me, but after a few weeks I'd move on, knowing that nothing would ever happen. I turned back to the internet, answering advertisements on craigslist. Most of the men I found were too far away to meet up with; the others wouldn't send photographs, or turned out to be far older than they said.

After a while, though, I found a man who lived not far away, and who had a car. He was older than me – I can't remember how old, but I'd guess now that he was in his early thirties and I was about sixteen. I couldn't invite a stranger to my parents' house, of course, and I didn't want to be seen out in public with a man I had no excuse for seeing. So we arranged to meet one night after dark on a lamplit path at the side of my village's football club. He didn't know the area, but I did. There was a tree-covered alley opposite that path, and I knew there were no lights in the alley. I figured I could wait there, in the darkness, hidden – I could see who this man was without him seeing me, and then I could decide what I was going to do next.

I remember walking out of the house and up the street, on to the canal bridge, and standing there looking down at the still, black water, the moon quivering on its surface, and thinking how stupid I was being. This could be the night I was killed – I might be found dead in a field, or my body might turn up in the boot of a car abandoned on a country road. The police would read my emails, would talk to my parents, and this would be how I was remembered, this was the thing that would be put in the papers. 'HIGH SCHOOL STU-DENT MURDERED BY OLDER MAN HE MET FOR OUTDOOR sex.' And yet my feet kept on walking, despite my better judgement. My body was coursing with a cocktail of hormones – I was desperate to meet someone, to touch someone, to let that buried part of myself out into the open. It needed to live. I needed to live.

I checked that no one was around on the street before I ducked quickly into the dark alleyway that would come out opposite our meeting point. I walked in the pitch black, my hand held up over my forehead to push back the over-hanging branches, but I had gone down this alley many times and knew its turns, and could sense my progress by the changing levels of the fences of the gardens that backed on to it and by the fences of the fields on the other side. When I neared the end, I could see the road ahead, the five-bar gate, and then the lamplit path across from me, stretching out behind the football club and up towards the woods.

I stared at the cone of light from the lamp, the circle of brightness it cast across the narrow pathway and the haw-thorn and beech hedges that bordered it. It was like a stage set – I stood in the dark, opposite, my breathing shal-low and uncontrollably rapid, my knees shuddering, as I waited for the man to walk into the light. After a short while a small red car rounded the bend and passed by the path slowly. I heard it stop further up the road, and then I heard the sound of the car door opening and slamming shut. Then, footsteps.

The man who walked through the gate was tall and slim. He wore jeans and a hoodie. His head was hunched down, but his shoulders were broad and steady. He didn't pause under the lamp, but walked on down the path, perhaps looking for me, perhaps just not wanting to stand too close to the road. My breath was still catching in my throat and I was shaking. I inhaled deeply, trying to hold myself still. I weighed the life of that locked-away self against the risk to my other self, this other life I was living; and this time I found the first was stronger, more wilful. And so I walked across the road, unbarred the gate and decided, just this once, to let that other self – to let myself – live.

*

Over the years, I did this many times, repeating the same ritual. I would hide and wait for the man to appear, and some-times I would go forward, and other times I would slink off back down the dark path and walk home with a sense of relief. Every time I swore to myself it was the last time; but inevitably, maybe a month later, that other self would start shaking its cage inside me, becoming more urgent, until finally I let it free. As time passed, I felt a sense of control out there – I knew the pathways through the fields, knew where the brook was liable to flood over, where the ground gave way, which parts of the hedgerow were thinned and easy to pass through, where the clearings were between the trees. Because I always met people in the same place, it felt as though I was the host, welcoming them into a world I knew, walking off into the night with the sound of their footsteps following behind. Because there was nowhere else for me to go, I made a secret sort of home out there.

I thought, during those years, that I was the only person who had discovered this possibility of the night-time and of the woods and fields that ringed the edges of our suburb. Of course, that wasn't true. Every town has its nooks, its aban-doned plots, its playing fields. In fact, not long ago I looked into the archives of our local newspaper, and it was curious to see how often there were reports of men 'loitering' in lay-bys down the small roads on the outskirts or, it appeared, even closer to home in the public toilets in the village. Amongst articles on gay-bashing, hate crimes, angry letters about the lowering of the age of consent between two men (with all the attendant insinuations of paedophilia), I noticed a number of articles reporting complaints from residents about 'undesirable activities' – men hanging around in the churchyard near to the bus stop I used to alight from on the way to school.

The police sergeant warned in the paper that 'Any person caught engaging in such activities can be arrested and have charges for gross indecency brought against them.' Even though the crime of 'gross indecency' was removed from the law in 2003, perhaps it was lucky I never found these places. Still, it wasn't only public toilets. One article from the early 2000s referred to 'perverts' (two men having consensual sex) in a park. Another reported that 'gay porn sites' were listing a number of locations across the town where men could meet each other: the town hall gardens, Bank Park, the market hall. The 'venues', the newspaper said, were even 'given an individual star rating' along with information about 'peak times'. 'Even particular bushes' were given write-ups. I wondered which of Bank Park's pink hydrangeas came out on top.

All these places I used to walk past, or walk through, and I never knew a thing. There was so much silence. The town I grew up in, in the north-west of England, sat astride the muddy waters of the River Mersey. It had an air of former grandeur: a golden gate in front of a stately town hall, Victorian public parks, grand buildings that were now home to charity shops and discount supermarkets. Near the centre, a soap and detergent factory sent a constant flow of steam from cooling towers, and the high street was ramshackle, the shops never seeming to survive long before lack of business shut up their doors. It was a big town, sprawling out into the countryside, and all the surrounding villages (like the one I lived in) had blurred their boundaries over the years and been swallowed into it. Years before, it had been a manufacturing hub, thriving on wire, steel and chemical production, but gradually the industries had left and were replaced by call centres and warehouses for impersonal corporations.

Still, despite the town's size, I didn't know anyone there who was gay. I didn't even know anyone who knew anyone who was gay. There was no Queer Night to go to, no discussion of queerness at school, apart from through rumours and bullying. Boys of my generation, born in the late Eighties or early Nineties, grew up in a febrile, uncertain, and still hostile atmosphere. We were born during the most deadly years of the AIDS epidemic, but came of age after the tide had begun to turn. Even so, that history was embedded into us through a series of hints and warnings. At school, Section 28 meant that teachers couldn't 'promote' homosexuality, which meant that it was never discussed at all. What I was left with was this unsettling feeling that we didn't exist, or that there were so few of us I'd never find another person like me. I knew I didn't exist alone – there were the men I met, after all – but I existed alone among the people I knew, the people I loved. Although there were moments of visibility on television or in music, things I looked out for secretively, trying not to show too much interest, all these instances seemed to be met with the lash. Popstars and actors would come out, and the media furore and the discussions I overheard were a warning to me not to do the same. I sensed it, and then I watched it happen. I stood at the edge of the path, staring towards the light, and then I turned and I walked myself back.

*

Not long ago, rooting through boxes at my parents' house, I found a poem I had written when I was about eighteen or nineteen. The usual teenage stuff, perhaps, and not very good, but it struck me, when I discovered it, like something I had forgotten. I recognised the boy who had written it. I had lost him in the meantime and was grateful for this trace of his existence. The poem was called 'My Twin Brother'. In it I had invented an identical twin. He was the one people loved; he was the one who was popular; he was the one whose every move I tried to imitate. In the poem, I killed him. It was violent and I had revelled in its gory images: the knife drawn across the skin of the throat, me lugging his body down the stairs, his head knocking on each step. At the end, I dragged the body into the street, so everyone could see what I had done. They were horrified, and I was free. I had killed him. He needed it. I needed it. Everywhere I went, he was there, in front of me. I had kept him alive while I could, but in the end, the bastard needed to go. If I hadn't done it, he would have killed me instead, I was sure.

Sometimes I wonder how thorough I was; how thorough it is possible to be. Is he still there, in the back of my mind, saying things to me, speaking on my behalf? Am I still mimicking, still living in his shadow? Sometimes, still, I feel haunted by a part of myself. Meeting men at night, all those years, I let the ghost inside me out. It seemed right to me when I learned that 'haunting' used to be slang for cruising; 'ghost' for a closeted gay man. There's something purgatorial about it, and something tantalisingly otherworldly. 'I am the ghost of Shadwell Stair,' wrote Wilfred Owen, becoming a ghost inside his own poem, hiding enough of himself that his readers might only guess what he meant when he wrote of a shadow walking along the moonlit Thames to the sound of shipping clanks and water.

> I walk till the stars of London wane
> And dawn creeps up the Shadwell Stair.
> But when the crowing syrens blare
> I with another ghost am lain.

And here I was, nearly a hundred years later, doing the same thing. I didn't learn it from anyone – I thought I was the first man in the world to have discovered it. How could it be that I carried that history inside myself, some instinctive urge pulling me out of the house at night? Blake's aphorism: 'The bird a nest, the spider a web, man friendship.' Perhaps that was it. And it was friendship I discovered there: the men were kind to me, there was a camaraderie to it, a kinship. I think I was lucky to have found them.

By some instinct, when the world had blocked my path, I went out and made a new one; and it happened that the one I made was already there, already marked out by others, only it was invisible to me, as though all those men were speaking through me, moving me, haunting me, guiding me on. Perhaps that is why I feel so close to them, a sort of familial closeness – where they went I followed, and the further I went, the more I felt them watching over me. As I moved forward, I also moved back, looping history inside myself, listening to them, communing with them. When I could not speak to anyone, I spoke with them.

*

Still, I was plagued by a sense of my own guilt. It wasn't just the community of these strangers I had drawn from. Like a tree, infolding all the years of its growth, registering the weather and the seasons in its body, in its shape and its knotted form, I had embodied my years, too. I had taken inside myself all of the things I had heard and seen, all of the ways I had been treated. How could I not have dealt them back? How could I not have enacted in my life the things that had been acted on to me? How many of my own hurts had I embodied and played out again in my life, passing the same things on to others?

When things with Elias began to rupture more often into arguments, I would leave the apartment and sit on a bench somewhere, and I would turn through the drudge of the past, picking out each hurtful word I had ever said to him, each unkindness I had committed against him, and I would accuse myself with them. There were nights when I convinced myself I had caused it all, that at the centre of the torn world was me – every sharp, unthinking criticism, every selfish thing I had done, each of them a small cut in the fabric, slicing away until eventually it ripped apart. I began to see all the meanness of the world clustered into myself, as though I were conducting the charge of it through me, concentrating it into a lethal energy.

In the ways I had chosen to hide, to integrate, I had embodied over the years the harmful structures of the world. When I first came out, I distanced myself from other queer people; I insisted to friends and family that I was not

like them. I was *normal* – a mantra I repeated over and over
to myself. I was good, and good meant not queer. So even
though I was queer, I lived adjacent to myself. I distanced
myself from myself long after I had come out, long after I
was apparently engaged in the daily ritual of *being me*. But
it wasn't enough to distance myself from myself. I had to
distance myself from the incriminating aspects of other
people, too. If I were to go under the radar, even when
ostensibly that wasn't what I was doing any more, I had to
be perfect, and I had learnt, by that stage, what perfect
meant in the world around me.

I met the first boy I dated properly at a club in my home
town. I was at university then, but had come home for the
December break. It was an after-hours bar, the sort of place
people went when all the other clubs had closed. Drinks cost
£1 each and the entry fee was cheap. Inside, the dance floor
was thronged with lights, the fog from a fitful smoke machine,
and drunk couples groping each other. I saw him walk past
me: jet-black hair, thick eyebrows, and bright green eyes
bloodshot with drink. I smiled at him, but he didn't see me. I
thought he was heading outside for a cigarette, so I stumbled
out a few minutes later, pretending I needed some fresh air,
and there he was, standing at the mouth of the alleyway next
to the bar, where the dustbins were lined up.

A man came out of the back door, threw some bottles
into one of the bins with a sharp ringing crash, and then
went back inside. I went over to the boy, and asked him if I
could borrow a cigarette. He took the packet from the
pocket of his jeans, shaking with the cold, offered me one,
and then, as I lifted it to my lips, he clicked his lighter, and I
held my hands cupped around it, puffed and exhaled. He
had a strong accent – the same accent I would have had if I

hadn't worked so hard to get rid of it over the years. By that point I was intoxicated by him: he had a slight frame, an effeminacy which seemed at odds, to me, with the drawn-out vowels and gutturals of his voice.

We talked for a while. We were laughing at how much each of us was shaking. It was a clear night – one of those where you can almost feel the heat being drawn up into the deep, empty sky – and before long we decided to go back inside. The bar was a blur of bodies, and as we moved through them I felt him hold back, brushing against me. I left my hand loose at my side, willing him to take it, to touch me, but he didn't. I couldn't find my friends, and neither could he – the dance floor wasn't so much a place where people were dancing, but a place where all the bodies were pushing, the rhythm of the music moving the whole crowd in sways. Once or twice he fell into me, and we laughed, and then, when he went to hold himself steady, I felt his fingers brush against mine, and he looked at me for just a split second longer than usual, those green eyes staring right into my own.

He came close to my ear and I bent towards him.

'Shall we go outside?' he said, but the music was too loud. I couldn't hear him, so he just tugged at me and I followed. By that point, I would have followed him anywhere.

Moments later we were back walking down the alleyway at the side of the bar. It was quiet, though you could still hear the pulse of the bass through the wall. He took my hand and pulled me towards him, and we hid behind the bins so that no one could see us. It was a rough town – there was always fighting outside the bars, stories of stabbings in the local paper, people being smacked senseless by bouncers in the backrooms of the clubs off the high street. Not a wise place to be caught kissing another boy after dark, but we couldn't help it.

A few weeks later, when I introduced him to some friends, one of them took me aside. Surely I wasn't serious about him? He was beautiful, I said. Kind, funny. I sensed, though, that my friend's objection was to his accent, and to his campness. He drew attention to himself, and it gave them an idea of his class, his education. That friend, and others over the next month or two, questioned me, again and again, never seriously, but casually. Still, the repetition began to eat into me. I wasn't doing it right. I wasn't being normal. He was a liability. In the end, I thought perhaps they had a point. What did we have in common?

So, with blunt force, I told him one night, over a video call. I repeated their concerns as if they were my own. In fact, they had become my own. I took on that homophobia, that classism, and I made it my own. I heard their words, and I dealt them out to him, and watched him start to cry. When I closed the laptop, I sat in the quiet of my room and felt, again, that I was safe.

How many times had I done this with Elias? How many times had I squirmed at his exuberance, afraid of him bringing us to the attention of straight people? How many times had I criticised him or shown my embarrassment? What had I passed on to him, what hurt had I caused? What if everything, all of it, was me? My anger, my guilt, was so strong that I felt it inside my body, a living thing squirming beneath my skin, and I wanted to claw it out.

*

After that night at the ice rink, my friends went back to London, never having met Elias, and the two of us struggled on alone in our studio apartment, our secret intact. By the time we reached 'the year's midnight' – St Lucy's Day – I was broken. It had only been a few months since Elias's birthday, but the cycles of hope and despair came with such repetitiveness, and with such disorientating irregularity, that I had lost all anchorage. Some days, things seemed to improve, but most came and went with little change. While Elias was trapped inside himself, I had become empty, numbed, and couldn't face returning to the world. I had confided in only one of my friends; from everyone else I had kept the details of my life secret for so long that I couldn't imagine how I could go back to the before-time, or how I could exist among people who didn't know what had happened. The shock of the event never seemed to leave, so after the initial steeling rush, my mind hid itself away in a vacuum where nothing much could happen. For a long time I was blocked off from feeling, from attachment, from articulation. I pushed myself aside, willingly, to try to help. It was only afterwards, when I went looking for myself again, that I found I did not know where that self had gone.

That St Lucy's Day, I wanted to trust the darkness, to trust the turning of the year, to feel the metaphor of the seasons as redemptive. I had booked a flight home for Christmas, just a week away, and Elias's parents told me they would look after him, and although I couldn't trust that he would be safe, I was so exhausted that I found myself wanting to escape. If I left, if only for four or five days, the worst might happen. But every hour I remained, I poured more and more of myself away. I did not know how long I could survive the staying.

In Gothenburg, the wildness of the sub-zero weather made the outside world feel inhospitable. For Elias and I, there was still love, but it was a grasping, difficult love. On my side, it flashed more easily now into resentment. I felt

trapped and afraid, held hostage to unpredictability; and
then I felt guilty, selfish and inadequate, incapable of the
care that was being asked of me, the care I wanted to give.
On the morning of St Lucy's Day, I lay in bed, hungover,
and scrolled through my phone. A friend had posted John
Donne's 'Nocturnal', a poem I hadn't read for years.

> Oft a flood
> Have we two wept, and so
> Drown'd the whole world, us two; oft did we grow
> To be two chaoses . . .

In a spirit of reconciliation, we had planned to go to the
cathedral for the Lucia service. Before the calendars were
changed, *Luciadagen* always fell on the winter solstice. We
queued outside the cathedral that afternoon in the pale,
blue-grey in-between, as the day tilted on its slow axis, the
sky turning pewter above us. People stood around drinking
mulled wine from paper cups. There were families with
children, grandparents, all of them reuniting, coming into
the city to gather in the church.

Unlike the gothic expanse of Liverpool's cathedral,
Gothenburg's was classical and clean. Inside, the walls were
plastered and painted a warm cream, and there were marble
pilasters with motifs in gold leaf clustered and unfurling
above the large, clear-glass windows. When Elias and I
entered, the light was muted and candles glowed weakly
around the altar. As the rest of the congregation filed in
around us, taking their pews, hustling together to make
room, the room grew gradually darker inside, so that by the
time the hush fell over the people, the small flames seemed
to have grown in intensity. The lights dimmed further, and

there was a soft, slow carol, gently held aloft by a solo piano. I looked furtively across my shoulder to see if Elias was singing next to me, to see if he knew the words. In all that quiet harmony, I found that I could not make out his voice.

From the back of the church, and down the aisle, came a procession of boys and girls in long white gowns. Some wore tall hats blazoned with stars, and at the front a blonde girl with a red sash around her waist wore on her head a wreath of evergreen leaves and a crown of candles. Their light, moving and dimming as she walked, seemed to invite the gold leaf around the church to flicker, as though it had been brought briefly to life. The singing was so peaceful, its melodies lifting in clear harmonies, that it had the effect of buoying my body.

Then, when the song quietened, and all the boys and girls in their white gowns gathered around the altar, the priest, in a low and steady tone, called to St Lucia: *Kom med det ljus som skingrar mörkret inom oss.* 'Lucia, bring the light that dissipates the darkness within us.' This year, more than any before, I felt the need of that ritual, of the candle and the lantern, to follow their wading light. Elias and I stood together, not touching, our faces burning as the blood warmed against our skin; and as the girls and boys began a second hymn, the gentle piano accompanying the glow of the candles and their warm high voices, I thought that perhaps a symbol of hope, even if it were not the real thing, might take hope's place, might masquerade long enough to matter.

*

For three years or more after that, Elias and I found our path. Things got better. Still, there was so much that I had buried, so many things I had silenced along the way. I was a different person afterwards, irrevocably changed. I found that I was not in control of myself. I drank more, I smoked more, I saw less of friends. I stayed up late at night on my own, numbing myself. I didn't have the energy for my life, or for us. I felt that I had given everything, and could not give any more. I rented out a room back in Liverpool and, early one December, when he was visiting me in England, we admitted finally that some things could not be fixed.

It was inevitable, and my grief came from the confirmation, the utterance, of things I knew could not be changed. Afterwards, the two of us walked down into Liverpool city to meet my parents. The day was dark blue, metallic, and the wind was full of knives that cut across us. We had tickets for Handel's *Messiah* at the Philharmonic. When we sat down in the concert hall and the lights lowered and the orchestra tuned up, I thought I wouldn't make it through to the end. On one side, my father, looking up patiently at the stage, his coat folded over his lap. On my other, Elias.

Then, after the sinfonia, when the music paused, and the stage seemed to glow with the warm echoes of the strings, the tenor walked to the front in his suit and his bow tie, and sang 'Comfort Ye, My People'.

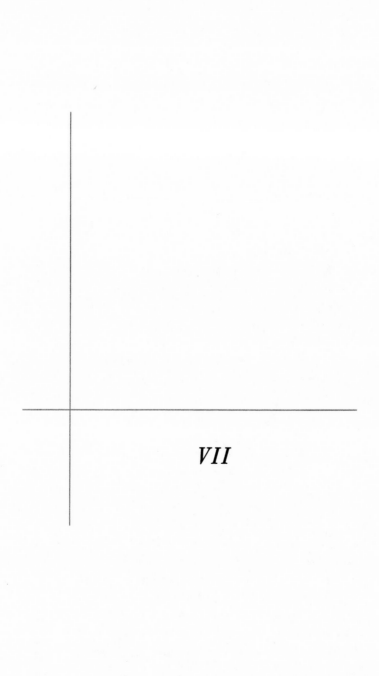

VII

Back in Liverpool, lonely after Elias had left, and not at home with myself, I brought man after man to my room. Each of them offered a brief distraction, a momentary eclipse of the mind. One time, it was the novice priest I met, but there was no shortage of others. Afterwards, feeling momentarily buoyed or ashamed, I kept to walking at night. Long walks along the river path or through the parks. I passed the cathedral often, and the docks. Once I walked down to look for the depth gauge which Elias had loved on the embankment, half-expecting to find that the tide had washed it away altogether.

Other times I would walk through the endless streets of terraces, losing my way in the angular turns of the roads, following the patterns of the street names until they changed. There was a group of streets named after Welsh towns; another cluster named after the novels of Sir Walter Scott. Mostly, I followed the slope of the city down to the waterfront, but one evening, when I hadn't seen anyone for days, I walked to the north of the centre, crossing the Islington road, looking for the St Francis Xavier Church, where Hopkins had delivered his sermons. I could see the tall spire from at least a mile away, but I took the longer route. Queen Anne Street, where Hopkins had watched the farriers at their forges, was now cornered with a bowling shop and backed on to by warehouses. There were no streetlights and it was late, so I walked quickly through, reaching the playing field at the other side and taking a right. The streets: Harker, Soho, Langsdale. I couldn't get the order of them.

When I approached the church, I was surprised. Not by the building itself, not by its yellow stone and sharp, thin spire, nor by its size. I'd read that in its heyday there were regularly between five and six thousand members of the congregation, and the church struggled for capacity. What I was surprised by was the total ordinariness of its surroundings: the houses on the streets around had been knocked down since the church was built, and they had been replaced with a modern estate, with little cul-de-sacs and square front lawns. When Hopkins was here, the church was surrounded by terraces and tenement slums. I realised I had wanted it to be a pilgrimage; I had wanted the houses to look like the houses he would have walked amongst. But then, I knew, those houses were dank, overpopulated, not fit for the people who lived in them. What I wanted for my dream, and what those people deserved, were two different things altogether. There was beauty in the ordinariness, in the reality, in the dignity of it.

As I approached the church it seemed to grow higher and higher, the angle of my sight getting steeper as it loomed over me, and the form of it seemed to imprint itself on me, so I felt its imposition, its shadow inside myself, as though it were a living thing, as though it remembered. I came because I wanted to be close to the man who I felt had spoken to me. I wanted to be ministered to, to confess, to be absolved. I wanted, feeling lost, to be found.

For weeks, thinking of Sweden, trying to make sense of

it, I had been reading Hopkins's sermons when I could not sleep. They were strange, sometimes forceful and moralistic, other times full of comfort. There were guardian angels, Hopkins said, who watched over us. 'We who are so full of the miseries of the flesh that we cannot bear at times to be in each other's presence are watched without ceasing by these glorious beings.' Perhaps he was watching me now, his words guiding me through the darkness he himself had not survived. I believed that not because I thought it was true, but because I wanted it to be true. I wanted to find hope, or a narrative, or a grander meaning.

The shrubs around the church started to hiss with rain as I approached. I stood at the iron railings, holding them, my hands tight with the cold. A door opened and closed in the estate behind me; a car moved slowly along the road, then turned a corner and was gone. I could picture Hopkins inside the church, in the smoke of incense, the light of the stained glass across his face, the massive congregation listening to him speak. I thought, then, that perhaps the strength of his faith was garnered from his losses, his isolation. He needed, more than most, something to believe in, something to make living worthwhile.

There was one word I had kept coming back to in his sermons over those past weeks, and I was thinking about it as I stood there outside the place where he had delivered them. The word was 'paraclete'. Hopkins spoke of Christ's body, his beautiful form, his strong limbs, 'moderately tall, well-built and tender in frame'. 'I make no secret,' he told his listeners, 'I look forward with eager desire to seeing the matchless beauty of Christ's body in the heavenly light.' Where he had to make a secret of his desire for other men, his longing for Christ's body could be shared, and was all the more feverish for the impossibility of attaining it. In one of the sermons, Hopkins spoke about the Holy Ghost, figured as a dove, a comforter, a paraclete. 'It must be in the face of difficulties, hardships, resistance . . . that he cheers us on.' If he had put together Christ and Dolben – their bodies laid over each other, a shame displaced into worship, a double exposure of longing and reverence – it made sense to me then that all of these lost men and women could be my paracletes, my watching ghosts. For a paraclete is 'one who encourages, stirs up, urges forward, who calls us on' – 'What the spur and command is to a horse, a Paraclete is to the soul.'

*

As I turned away from the church and took my long walk home through Liverpool, I was spurred on, feeling as though, once again, I had found my guide, the ghost who understood me. But as my steps continued, down again into the city, I couldn't keep hold of the image there. If I was being spurred on, I still had no idea where I was supposed to go. I was due to visit my parents' house, taking the last train later that night so I could spend Sunday with the family. I knew that I would ruin it for myself, and for them, being hungover, tired, sad, but it was ruined anyway, and it felt easier to have a day ruined because of something I was responsible for – a headache or vomiting – than to have it ruined because my world, my life, felt ruined.

When I got back to the apartment, my housemates were drinking in the kitchen. I had told myself I wouldn't drink any more, but I couldn't help it. I sat at the old dining table and as the hours passed I drank so much wine that I couldn't focus any more. I cried in front of everyone and didn't even have the wherewithal to feel ashamed. I rolled cigarette after cigarette and smoked them by the open door. The wind blew the smoke back inside and it stung my eyes and floated in a blue fog under the ceiling light. At some point I took a few drags of my friend's weed. Predictably, my brain fizzed and the room started to turn and I felt nauseous. I stumbled to the bathroom, tripping over my own legs. After throwing up in the toilet, and flushing it, I turned on the tap, lifting shaky palmfuls of water to my lips, rinsing the acid and the vomit from my mouth. I looked up at the mirror. My eyes were bloodshot, my skin yellowed and pale. I was too drunk to care what I looked like. I wiped my mouth on the back of my wrist, pulling out a sling of phlegm, then washed my hands with soap.

The last train from Lime Street was at half-past eleven, but I had no idea what time it was now. I steadied myself against the doorframe and checked my watch. It was much earlier than I thought, but I couldn't drink any more. When I went back into the kitchen and told my friends I had to go, they offered to call me a taxi. I didn't know if I could survive the backseat of a car without throwing up again or passing out, so I said no, I'd prefer to walk. I needed the fresh air to sober me up; I needed to find my balance again. I held on to the banister as I put on my boots, pushing my foot into each one clumsily, my head lolling, my eyes drifting off. I put on my old second-hand Gant coat, and my rucksack, then patted my pockets to check I had everything. 'Wallet. Keys. Presbytery keys?'

Outside, the orange street lamps shone through the dark. The car park was silent, and I walked between the potholes, taking a cigarette from behind my ear and lighting it. The road was a long boulevard with a pathway down the centre. Copper beeches that still hadn't lost their leaves swayed their arms above me. There was a group of kids smoking around some benches – I put my headphones on and kept my eyes down, not wanting to draw attention to myself. I couldn't hear if they said anything as I passed, but I kept walking anyway, not turning around to check. I passed the synagogue and the mosque and orthodox church with its golden dome, and then crossed into the Georgian streets, which were quiet, too, but brighter because of the passing cars. I still had an hour before the train left.

Then the thought struck me to walk down into the cathedral gardens again, like I had a fortnight after Elias left. Perhaps that man, the kickboxer, would be there, and would distract me for a while. I could see the top of the tower above the rooftops – a darker indigo against the dark sky – and made my way through the streets towards it. When I reached the fence, and the cathedral was before me, the moon was shining a strong white light over the gardens, bathing the trees, but still the deep recess of the cemetery was in shadow, so although I could peer down into it, I could only peer down into blackness. My eyes couldn't focus and they strained from trying to make out the forms below. It was so dark that the moon had printed itself on to my vision, and its white circle seemed to move across my closed eyelids in a sea of red.

I gripped on to the fence, suddenly feeling nauseous again, and my rucksack slipped along my arm as I leant forward. Time to keep moving. Turning right, in the direction of the city, I took the road on its downward slope towards the Mersey. As I rounded the corner, the wind smacked into me. I doubled down, leaning into it. It was like a hurry of bodies, all pushing past me – their hands blustering around my coat, trying to open it, grabbing on to my legs and pulling them, rushing around me and through me, blowing my mind clean. Then, quite abruptly, the wind slowed and the street seemed to exhale. A few birds swooped down and landed on the railings again, and the trees sighed and then settled, exhausted from the battering.

As I turned on to the small square in front of the cathedral, with the Oratory behind the fence, a rag of cloud slipped over the moon, hiding it for a moment before the wind pulled the cloud away again. I felt comforted to see that the moon was still there, unmoved, unwavering. In front of the Oratory door, I could see, was a tall rod, about four metres high, and a tiny bird, like a starling, was perched on top of it. How had I not noticed it before? I steadied myself against the railings and watched it. There were no stars that night, but I thought of the starling's wing, its patterned breast, the flecks of white against the black feathers, as though the heavens might have constelled into it, readying themselves for flight. Then, after looking a long while at it, I realised that it wasn't a real bird at all. It didn't flinch with the wind. It didn't ruffle itself for warmth. It was made of metal – bronze, perhaps – like a Roman standard, a totem, but not a symbol of war, not an eagle or a horse, just a small, speckled bird. I looked up at the great tower of the cathedral, its statue of Christ high above the main door, and then back to the bird, following the line of sight.

When I carried on to the sloping path into the cemetery, I stood at the threshold, looking down to that sunken place. The grave-lined tunnel, the shapes of the trees narrowing in the far distance into a complete blackness, and somewhere beyond it, I knew, the moon-bathed stillness of the statuary and the monuments and the spring. But, standing there, it was as though something had changed in me now; something, or someone, seemed to hold me back. Where I had felt, before, the draw of that path, its tide pulling me almost outside of my body, I felt now as though there were an invisible force halting me, keeping me in place. I could see the path, and I could picture the gardens beyond and almost hear the sound of the spring in its constant high-pitched falling, but I was frozen still. My feet were heavy and my mind was too tired to overcome the weight of my body. No matter how much I willed it, I couldn't walk forward. I could feel myself buckling from the inside, as though I might crumple inwards around an absence.

Shivering in my coat, still drunk and incoherent, even to myself, I found that I was no longer the man that could walk alone at night in the gardens, amongst the gravestones, with the sound of the water tinkling into the pool below. Where before I was still in shock, or perhaps braced by the idea that the worst had already happened, now, everything had turned again, everything seemed once again like a threat. Too much had been proven. I'd lost the confidence to think I was above things, apart from the world, that what had happened to others wouldn't happen to me. In there – in the gardens just out of view – that was the world of another man, and I had lost his bravery or his disregard. I had lost, too, the desire for what is dangerous, the thrill of the unexpected. When I lost the safety of the world, I lost the safety of my own body, and I couldn't bring myself to overcome it.

I took myself, finally, right down to the edge of the stone passage, just far enough that I could see the light of the moon on the gardens beyond the trees; and I was glad just to see it, to have a glimpse into that world, that past. As a teenager, I would have walked easily into the darkness, and in times of shock, I seemed to revert back, to play out those earlier habits. Now, though, all that was changed. I wasn't numb enough to go back, and not confident enough either. But just as I was about to leave, to turn around and take the roads through the city to the station, the wind picked up again, blowing up from the river and hurrying down into the gardens. I closed my eyes, steadying myself against it, and this time the wind was behind me, lifting my collar, billowing my coat. I kept my eyes closed, the gusts blustering around my head, until it felt for a moment as though I were not alone, and it felt as though there were other people, their shadows moving at either side of me, gathering around me, lifting me forwards, bearing me with them.

I opened my eyes again and looked around. If I stared down into the cemetery, the glow of the street lamps behind me, and called out, what would come to me? Would the statues in the Oratory wake? Would the graves begin to rupture? Was anybody there? And if there was, would I recognise any of them if they came out of that darkness and stepped towards me? What if it was myself, or that lost version of me, a flicker of the past – would I know his face, and would he know mine? All that time I had been haunted by him, and still I hardly knew what that self was, that version of me that existed before the world had said *become*, and I had answered in its language.

I thought of Hopkins, his line of men walking in the marsh air with their beams, following a lantern. At the end of the poem it is Christ who watches them, whose heart wants them, whose care haunts them, 'Their ransom, their rescue, and first, fast, last friend.' And then I remembered one of the last poems Karin Boye ever wrote. Elias and I had translated it together. In the poem, she also followed a procession, this time of women, 'dark angels with blue flames / like fire-flowers' in their hair:

De mörka änglarna med blå lågor
som eldblommor i sitt svarta hår
vet svar på underliga hädarfrågor –
och kanske vet de var spången går
från nattdjupen till dagsljuset –
och kanske vet de all enhets hamn –
och kanske finns det i fadershuset
en klar boning, som har deras namn.

Those dark angels with blue flames
like fire-flowers in their black hair
know the answers to blasphemous questions –
and perhaps they know where the bridge goes
from the depths of night to the day –
and maybe they know the harbour of unity –
and maybe, in the father's house, there is
a bright dwelling that has their name.

Both of them hoped – one with certainty, one with longing – that there would be a place for those people, a friend to watch them, a room with their name above the lintel. But perhaps, after all, it should never be another place, never be another person. It should be here, the friends should be us, the father's house should be our own. Standing at the foot of that pathway, I realised that maybe that was it, after all. Maybe I could call to them, could call to myself. In my body, in my deeds, in my words. I would set a fire burning for them, I would bring them home.

*

Two years later, I had gone to my family home again for the holidays. My father had died, and this was to be our first Christmas without him. All the things that usually brought joy to the house – the decorations, the carols, the family gathering together again – all of them were changed. The delicate, fragile quality of happiness, I learnt once more, was its briefness. This was to be the first year that we were no longer whole, no longer all together. So the music reminded us of happier times, and made us sad. Even cooking the dinner was mournful, knowing that someone else would be called on to carve the meat and that the chair at the head of the table would be empty. When finally I sat down beside my mother to eat, with all the holly and the Christmas crackers and the candles laid neatly across the table, I could see that empty chair out of the corner of my eye, and I could see my father sitting in it, with his paper hat and his glass of wine, smiling at me, and I wept.

After we had eaten, and raised a toast to absent friends, we sat by the fire in the living room. I stared into the flames, my eyes still hot and tender from the tears. There was a bowl of oranges by the fire, and a smaller bowl of cloves. Some of the oranges were already studded with them, the lines of cloves ringing the fruit. I took up one of the unstudded ones, pushing the nail of my thumb into the skin, feeling it give beneath the pressure. My mother was sitting on the sofa, a box of old photographs on her lap. I asked her to pass me some, and we both sat by the fire, hardly speaking, flicking through the images. Occasionally, she would pass one over to me, a holiday photo or a snap from a family party, pointing out someone's Eighties haircut, or saying how pretty someone used to be. After a while, she found baby photos, then my brothers and me, all in school uniform, standing in height order by the garden hedge. All the photos were taken by my father. In all of them we were looking at him, smiling at him, and now, holding the images, we were seeing ourselves through his eyes. For a short moment it felt as though I was him, that I was the father of these children, the father of myself, that he was inside me, that he wasn't gone at all.

I pushed my thumbnail again into the skin of the orange in my hand, smelling its fresh acid loosing out, and carried on looking through the box of photos. There was one of me with my face painted as a tiger. It was the only creature I would ever let them paint on my face at school fairs or at parties. The first poem I ever remember hearing, recited to me by my mother at my bedside, was one of William Blake's. 'Tyger, Tyger, burning bright / In the forests of the night, / What immortal hand or eye / Could frame thy fearful symmetry?' The part I loved best was in the final stanza, when 'could' changed to 'dare'. It gave me a thrill of fear, this creature that even God might be scared of. 'What immortal hand or eye / Dare frame thy fearful symmetry?' A challenge, a gauntlet thrown down – the celestial rain, the furnace, the anvil, the hammer. I would dream of those forges; the stoked fuel, the gloved hand.

Then, there were some photographs of a holiday in Stratford-upon-Avon. My parents had honeymooned there, and went back for their anniversaries. Sometimes, we went along too, my brothers and I. It's been a long time since I was there now, but I remember the little streets, the willows over the river, a sweet shop where I insisted on buying a woody stem of liquorice, which I spent the day chewing, pretending to like it, though the bark was dry and dusty. While my brothers ate their quarter of sherbet lemons, I chewed my way through the stick, and wouldn't admit that I had been wrong, wouldn't let down my guard.

I picked up my glass of wine and took a sip, edging my feet towards the fire. Then, as I flicked through more of the photographs, I came across one of myself, maybe five years old, staring right into the camera, with a turquoise and yellow caterpillar, thick as a bracelet, resting on the sleeve of my forearm. I knew I was looking up at my father, showing it to him. My eyes were big and disarmingly innocent. I felt that little boy looking at me, speaking to me, as if I were his father. Perhaps it is strange to say that I was confronted by my own innocence, but it felt as though I had come face to face with someone I had lost, someone who was watching me. I loved him. I loved him, and I felt the love inside me. It was like I had been shouting into the past and finally I had summoned him, that original self, and he was returning my gaze, my echo, as though to ask me what had happened. Hello, I thought. Hello, little one. It's been too long, hasn't it?

I remembered the day it was taken. We were inside a glasshouse by the river in Stratford. It was high summer and there were hundreds of butterflies in there. I had stood and watched them gather, like living jewels, around a table of fruits, amazed at the way the tiny croziers of their tongues would uncurl and drink from the nectar of the oranges. The air was thick with them, spiralling as though played by little flurries of wind. If I held out an arm, eventually one would land on it and petal me into stillness.

I loved to see how they mimicked the forms of the world on their wings – an ocellus, or the pattern of snake-print, all their gorgeous subterfuge. I had always wanted to be decorated like that, to hold out an arm and to have all the beauty of the world land on it, and make me beautiful, too. Looking at the photograph, I remembered something from Hopkins's letters – he had gone swimming and had put a sea anemone on to his forehead. 'I thought it would look strikingly graceful,' he said. The creature stung him, and left a large red scar on his skin.

Here I was with a caterpillar, thinking the same. I suppose I was always quick to learn the old theme – how one thing might hide itself in the cells of another, the elements broken down in the chrysalis, loosed and unmade, then regathering in mimicry and flying off. In the glasshouse, there were lupins, and honeysuckle clambered up metal frames; there were moths with pink masks, moths with olive fur. What I wouldn't have given to have something of their beauty, to be able to hide myself in all these forms, so I might shift, one moment, between a wood's or a river's camouflage, subsumed into the world, no longer separate from it.

In the month after my father died, before the real tide of grief hit me, I was struck by a sort of epiphany that replaced any lingering religious thought I had left. It wasn't that I lost faith (truly, by that point I didn't have much faith to lose); in fact, I gained faith, not in some god, but in the world around me. Before my father began the first of a brutal series of whole brain radiations, he had called me from the hospital. He and my mother had met with the consultant, and the consultant had laid out the facts as best she could. The radiation was needed – there was a high risk that the tumours in his brain would result in a stroke if they weren't dealt with now. There were several of them, and some of them were so small ('seeded', she said, throughout the tissue) that no more localised approach would work.

The problem was that, in the meantime, the other tumours in his body could not be treated, and so they would be left to grow and do further damage, while the radiation on his brain took effect. Only once those tumours were remitting could the others be dealt with, and by then it might be too late. The other risk of the whole brain radiation was that it might leave his brain damaged, less able to function. He might lose memory or some speech, and they didn't know if he would be able to regain it. He called me from the waiting room, his voice quiet, and I could hear how frightened he was, and I was frightened, too.

'All I want is my boys,' he said, his voice trembling, and I started to cry.

'I know, Dad, I know. I love you.'

'As long as I can still be with my boys, and can still sit in the garden and hear the birds. That's all I want.'

After he died, I thought of that often. The garden, the birds – that was his idea of heaven, a man who didn't believe in God, didn't know where he was going when he left. Really, that is the only heaven that makes sense to me, too.

When we buried him, we planted flowers on his grave, and every time I visited I saw that those flowers were my father, were made out of him. He was being born again into the earth, in a new form, and it wouldn't be long until all of his atoms were dispersed across the village, then the country, and then the world, carried off inside birds, growing into plants, and into butterflies. What was the garden, then, if not heaven, if not a place made up of everything that had been lost to us, if not an afterlife? After that, the whole world could be heaven to me. Still, it seems like the most simple, the most beautiful way I can think of looking at life. Everything, all of it, is mimicry.

Looking back at that photograph, I think that this is what I always knew, though I had forgotten it in the years between. It's not only matter that is folded and mimicked into new forms – time is folded into them, too. Everything carries within itself the remnant forms of older selves, older structures we have evolved through, vestiges of the history of our species. Every day, the present and the past coexist in the body. I think we carry those other histories, too, even before we know them. We speak with those ghosts all the time, even before we recognise who they are or what they are telling us.

But there was something else to the photograph, something I had never noticed before. I wonder if I knew at the time, but had forgotten? That caterpillar on my sleeve – it wasn't a butterfly's, but a moth's larva. From early childhood I had been obsessed with collecting creatures, caring for them, raising them. I had an ant farm, kept stick insects and butterflies, caught frogs and sticklebacks and water boatmen in the stream that ran through the village. I tried to give them a home in a makeshift pond that was really just a dustbin buried in our garden, filled with water. We still had the books I'd used to identify the creatures, and I took one down from the shelf across from my mother. She watched me as I lifted it down, but said nothing. The book – a guide to moths and butterflies – had hundreds of illustrations, all of the life cycles of the lepidoptera, and eventually I found that larva and smiled with the coincidence of it. It was the larva of a death's-head hawkmoth. Again, it seemed like I had been left a trace, a clue – that little boy, myself, holding up a symbol, staring up at his father, my father, and staring up at me. Still, still, like he wanted me to know.

The larva in the book was yellow-green, ridged along the top in chevrons of dusty, silver blue – and here it was, in the photograph, on my tiny, thin arm. I wonder if anyone had told me what it was that I was holding? Perhaps all I wanted to say was that it was beautiful and strange, and that I was beautiful like this, coloured and bright in the glasshouse. That caterpillar, the book said, would feed on the violet flowers of a nightshade, then, after a time, refigure itself and turn into a large damasked moth, brown and yellow, with a shape like a human skull marked on its thorax.

When I looked up the caterpillar in the book, I saw the Latin name for its imago: *Acherontia atropos*. Acheron, the mythic river of sorrow and pain, linked in myth's intractable grammar to Atropos, the Fate who held the thread of life between her shearing blades. Sorrow and the thread of life, and this little visitant from the inferno. When I looked up 'Acheron' on my phone, there was a short quotation from the eighth book of the *Aeneid*: '*flectere si nequeo superos, Acheronta movebo.*' 'If I cannot bend the will of heaven, I shall move hell.' Or maybe 'heaven' and 'hell' didn't work here. I searched for the translation and there were other suggestions, too. 'If I cannot move the powers that be, I shall move the river.' I didn't know which version was closer. Then I thought of Jack, all his dictionaries and glossaries and grammars stacked along the shelf in that room in Cambridge. He would have known. He would have sat me down and talked me through each possibility, all the sources of the words, all their inflections. If I cannot change the structures of the world, if I cannot bend the will of heaven, perhaps I can move the river, perhaps I can move hell. Whose heaven was it anyway?

That little boy stared at me from the photograph, his bright eyes looking up at me, the larva on his arm. What did I know then? What did that little boy know of the future? I knew one day that everyone would leave me – my parents, my friends – once I stepped out of the mimic of my body and told the truth. Always, through the haze of childhood, I heard a clock ticking down to the time when I would have to detonate the image of myself in front of them. I thought of the tawny markings on the insect's thorax, the two dark circles surrounded by lighter fur, which looked like a human skull, a 'death's head', and gave the creature its mythology as both an emblem and a warning. For a long time I had felt that inflexible Fate watching. I had seen the end of the thread, held between her fingers. I didn't know how long the thread was, but I had thought perhaps ten more years, or fifteen, was the best I could hope for. I say 'hope', because even though I was mimicking, even though I was hidden, and the hiding was crippling that fragile part of myself I knew to be true, I was also safe in my hiding. In my hiding, I was loved.

So I saw that everything else was in hiding, too, everything was connected, everything was metaphor. I saw the black leopard of the sky at night, or the tiger of the winter forest as the sunset glowed against the trees. It was all the parts of something else, remade. It was getting dark outside now and the flames in the grate whooshed and dimmed with the wind, then roared back. I thought of the boy in the photograph, that stranger the world had parted me from. What would I have been like if I had formed myself, if I had never had to integrate, if he was still here, one and the same with me? But no, there is no 'formed', only forming; ongoing, unfolding. I looked down at the photograph and saw the boy looking back at me. Little self-maker. Could I call him back, could I ask him to come home?

I unpeeled the orange in my hands, ribboning its thick hide into my palm. I put down the photograph on the arm of the chair, and leant forward and threw the rinds of the fruit one by one into the fire. They crackled and hissed as the flames hurried around them until the rinds began to curl and turn black. There were tiny sparks flying from the skin – they made a brief arc in the hearth as the acid leaked out, like some minor god, scattering stars. The wind rushed against the window and down the chimney, and the fire danced and crackled. I leant back into the chair and took a slow, deep breath. The smoke smelled first acrid, and then sweet.

BIBLIOGRAPHY

I have benefitted from numerous books and studies throughout the writing process. Foremost among these have been:

Margit Abenius, *Drabbad av renhet: en bok om Karin Boyes liv och diktning* (Bonniers, 1950)

Karin Boye, *Complete Poems*, trans. David McDuff (Bloodaxe, 1994)

———, *Samlade dikter* (Modernista, 2019)

Rob Cover, *Queer Youth Suicide, Culture and Identity: Unliveable Lives?* (Ashgate, 2012)

Digby Mackworth Dolben, *The Poems of Digby Mackworth Dolben, Edited With a Memoir*, ed. Robert Bridges (Oxford University Press, 1915)

Joseph J. Feeney, *The Playfulness of Gerard Manley Hopkins* (Routledge, 2008)

Éadaoín Lynch, 'As no men love for long: Wilfred Own and Siegfried Sassoon's intimate confederacy', *Times Literary Supplement* (6 November 2020)

Elaine F. Marshall, 'Hopkins's sermons and "Felix Randall": Responses to Hardship in His Urban Parishes', *Religion and the Arts*, Vol. 19 (2015), pp. 320–38

Robert Bernard Martin, *Gerard Manley Hopkins: A Very Private Life* (Flamingo, 1991)

Sally R. Munt, 'Gay shame in a geopolitical context', *Cultural Studies*, Vol. 33, No. 2 (2019), pp. 223–48

Walt Odets, *Out of the Shadows: Reimagining Gay Men's Lives* (Allen Lane, 2019)

Wilfred Owen, *The Collected Poems*, ed. C. Day Lewis, with a memoir by Edward Blunden (Chatto & Windus, 1968)

Johan Svedjedal, *Den nya dagen gryr: Karin Boyes författarliv* (Wahlström & Widstrand, 2017)

Matthew Todd, *Straight Jacket: Overcoming Society's Legacy of Gay Shame* (Black Swan, 2018)

Norman White, *Hopkins: A Literary Biography* (Clarendon Press, 1992)

The ongoing Oxford University Press edition of *The Collected Works of Gerard Manley Hopkins*, principally:

Vols 1 and 2: *Correspondence*, ed. R. K. R. Thornton and Catherine Phillips (Oxford University Press, 2013)

Vol. 3: *Diaries, Journals, and Notebooks*, ed. Lesley Higgins (Oxford University Press, 2015)

Vol. 5: *Sermons and Spiritual Writings*, ed. Jude V. Nixon and Noel Barber, S.J. (Oxford University Press, 2018)

'A Letter on Marriage from the President and Vice-President of the Bishops' Conference of England and Wales' was read to congregations in the Catholic parishes of England and Wales on 10 and 11 March 2012

Quotations are used from articles and correspondence published in the *Warrington Guardian*

ACKNOWLEDGEMENTS

First and foremost, I owe a debt of gratitude, admiration and the utmost respect to those people, other than myself, who are depicted in these pages. Thank you for your bravery, for trusting me, and for letting me write this book. I hope that I will be forgiven any misremembrances or indiscretions.

Names and identifying features have been wholly changed throughout this work in order to protect the privacy and anonymity of individuals. In some cases I have compressed timelines and changed geographies, merged two or more individuals into one, invented characters and altered or invented certain other details.

This book would never have been written without the unwavering encouragement, care and insight of my agent, Matthew Marland, to whom I owe a great debt of gratitude. I owe a significant amount to my two editors – Bea Hemming at Jonathan Cape and Caroline Sydney at Penguin Press – for their faith in me, as well as for their close, attentive and sensitive editorial work. Thanks, too, to Robin Robertson, who read early drafts of this work and offered insightful comments, editorial advice and encouragement. Thanks are also due to Adam Eaglin at The Cheney Agency, for his grace and support, and to Daisy Watt, Joe Pickering, Juli Kiyan, Jessie Stratton, Cecile Pin, Alison Davies, and the entire teams at Jonathan Cape and at Penguin Press.

Thanks to others who read early drafts and offered their feedback, and to those who discussed this book with me and offered their questions, their insight and their camaraderie: Andrew McMillan, Okechukwu Nzelu, Katie Mishler, Jake Erickson, Hussein Omar and Helen Tookey. For Nick, whose love and understanding has kept me afloat during the writing of this book, and for my family, who helped me through these pages as they were lived and as they were written.